Life Can Be a Miracle

Ivinela Samuilova

DEDICATION

For those who refuse to live their life as if it is something ordinary, a meaningless coincidence of circumstances, and for those who, despite the circumstances, continue to seek and uncover this miracle called - life.

CONTENTS

ACKNOWLEDGMENTS

I would like to thank Steve Szubert, Annie Alexieva and Alistair Turnbull who helped me to translate this story from Bulgarian into English.

Many thanks to my talented friend Nelly Lozanova for the beautiful and professionally designed book cover.

And many thanks to all those wonderful people who encouraged and supported me along the way.

1. CHAPTER ONE

The scattered line of people waiting suggested that a bus hadn't passed by for a long time. Yet, while she was buying a ticket, one arrived and, as expected, it was crowded. Fortunately, traffic was light and she reached her destination on time.

Adie hopped off the bus and let out a deep breath of triumph. She smiled, satisfied by the way she had just beaten that impudent old woman who was at the bus stop every morning. She knew the old dear's game inside out.

True to form, as the bus arrived, that mean creature, who seemed to be about 70, always dressed up and made up, dashed to the front with remarkably agility, roughly elbowing anyone who happened to be in the way. If there was a seat free, it would be hers.

Today, however, there were no empty seats. The old bat made no disguise of her fury at this. Her sharp elbows constantly engaged the ribs of anyone in her proximity. She spun round and round to ensure she missed no one. Everyone had to be included in her misery.

Indeed, on some days her usual performance was amusing to Adie. Yet, on other days the old bag simply jarred Adie's nerves.

Today, though, Adie saw the ideal opportunity to test a technique discussed at last night's seminar. She started to mentally mirror the old lady's behaviour. As she elbowed Adie, Adie nudged her in return: in her mind. As she trod on Adie's foot, Adie stepped on her foot: mentally. Blow by blow, as this mind game continued, the old lady calmed down until she was still, meek as a lamb.

Before getting off the bus, Adie visualised giving her a peck on the cheek, and mentally wished her a wonderful day. She imagined placing a necklace, her parting gift, around the old lady's neck. To her surprise, just as she was passing by her to get out of the bus, the impish woman, who until now had never taken the sullen look off her face, smiled widely at her.

"Ha! It really works!" Adie thought to herself and took off down the side path, sheltered by trees from the angry city traffic.

This path had a special significance for her. She called it 'the Magic Alley'. The two hundred meters she walked every day – from the bus stop to her work place - was a precious experience in her daily routine. Sometimes she thought it was worth keeping her present job, because she didn't want to lose these 10 magic minutes a day.

Though it was still early Autumn, the weather was already wintry cold and foul. But on Magic Alley the threads of fog only added an air of mystery to the enchantment that was always here, no matter the weather.

The wind swept a bunch of damp leaves and playfully swirled them around Adie.

"Hi, leaves!" Adie greeted them aloud and smiled, then quickly glanced around. "Phew!" No one was near to witness her greeting the dancing leaves. Adie laughed, imagining the possible reaction of a passerby. But this one wasn't as bad as the incident from yesterday morning. Recalling the episode made her burst out laughing.

The previous morning she had woken up in that low-spirited wretched mood that she could only naturalistically define as shitty. She couldn't understand why she had been waking up like that lately – tired, nervous and depressed instead of fresh and cheerful.

Sometimes she was quick to shake it off, but there were days when it lingered throughout her day, right up until she went to bed.

Yet, something funny happened yesterday. As she got off the bus and stomped down her Magic Alley, raging that she couldn't stand herself in this crappy mood, Adie stubbed her foot on something. She managed to skip as she stumbled, and somehow jumped over the obstacle rather than falling.

Producing the standard expletive for an accident like this, Adie looked back at the stone that had tripped her. But it was no stone; it was one impressively large and solid dog turd.

"I'm the shit jumper!" passed through her mind. Somehow, this new name she had spontaneously christened herself with sounded so funny and fitting her mood that she laughed out loud. In this absurd scenario, the personality which was irritated with everybody and everything all morning disappeared somewhere. Suddenly the whole wretched reality melted away and, for a moment, Adie even felt like she was attending a great universal party 'here and now' (or rather 'nowhere and never'). Precisely, the sensation she had was of a curious existence in some other reality.

When her awareness returned to this reality 'here and now', Adie put a hand on her mouth to suppress her laughter and looked around. It was all clear.

Still smiling, she did a quick "reality check", lifting each leg in turn to inspect the soles of her shoes. Clean: there were no visible traces of the incident. As she was returning her second foot to the ground, a gust of wind delivered a scrap of newspaper to her feet. Adie stepped on it. Her eyes flitted over the exposed part of the bold headline:

"ONLY 10 DAYS LEFT..."

She lifted her foot again to see "to what", but the teasing wind snatched the news away. Just at that moment her favourite Queen song filled the headphones of her MP3 player: It's A Kind Of Magic.

"Right on cue!" mused Adie, "but this is not just a kind of ... it's definite magic to be a good shit-jumper!" she giggled again.

Still giggling at the previous morning's incident, Adie put on her player, thinking: 'And what happened today with the old monster was like magic.' She pressed the button, certain that she was playing the same song. But what buffetted her ears was "Don't stop me now... I'm having such a good time..."

'Oh, that's an excellent choice!' – exclaimed Adie with a smile and, singing quietly, continued on her way.

The song ended just as Adie arrived at her workplace. Pulling off her headset, she sighed, and entered the turnstile.

3

Adie greeted the porter politely and headed for her office. There she said 'hello' to her colleagues, sat at her desk and turned on the computer.

The process of switching into work mode gave Adie a feeling of being something of a multiple personality. She sometimes wondered how her co-workers would react if they could witness the torment raging inside her soul and mind. They regarded her as serious person, even a little aloof. But they respected her.

Adie had moved from her small native town to the capital; one reason for having done so was the anonymity, which the city of millions provided. She did not welcome anyone getting too close. She preferred her private life to remain like this and cut off all attempts of familiarity right from the off, when she started working there.

She was aware that there were people who, behind her back, commented how 'secretive' she was, but she could live with that. This was mild compared to the small town, where people seemed to make sense of and fill the gaps in their own lives with all sorts of commentaries of the personal lives of others.

Thinking about her multiplicity, on impulse Adie googled 'multiple personality'. 2 600 000 results were instantly returned. "That's multiple," thought Adie.

She ran quickly through 2-3 pages and was not surprised to find out that it was a disorder. Its basic feature is the obvious existence of two or more clearly defined personalities in one person as, in any given moment, only one of them is apparent. Each of the personalities is padded out with his/her own memories, behaviour and predilections. There was even a second term for the disorder – Dissociative Identity Disorder. She clicked the link and giggled to herself as she read:

You may wonder if Dissociative Identity Disorder is real. Understanding the development of multiple personalities is difficult, even for highly trained experts. But Dissociative Identity Disorder does exist...

The article went on to insist that, naturally, the occurrence of this disorder must be related to some past traumatic experience.

Adie fumed at the ease with which experts invented endless disorders and offered them as diagnoses to convince people there is something wrong with them. And how they abused the term 'traumatic experience'... but just as bad was how naive people could be to allow these so-called 'specialists' to convince them they must be victims of something or someone.

Adie couldn't understand why no one had seriously questioned, for example, why the number of cases of women sexually abused by their fathers in childhood seemed to have mushroomed recently. How could half the fathers of little girls become such evil perverts so suddenly?

To Adie's mind, many people were being manipulated through supposed deeply buried (and conveniently forgotten) memories, and that was the real crime. In most cases the 'victims' had never gone through anything like what they were told they 'remembered'. If they were victims of anyone, it was of unscrupulous 'therapists'. "They're the real 'rapists' in these cases," she ruminated.

Adie stared at the monitor, eyebrows furrowed. To her workmates, she appeared to be engrossed in some seriously important work. But she was trying to resolve whether she was truly 'multiple' or whether she was only consciously like this? Or maybe she couldn't integrate the various 'Adies' within herself?

She knew her personality was inconsistent, that's why she didn't like defining herself or being 'labeled'. 'Good', 'bad', 'mature', 'adventurous', 'tender', 'rude', 'tactful', 'vulgar', 'loving', 'hating', 'funny', 'boring' …Adie realized she flitted between all of these, and more. And when she was one of those, she was that "person" 100 percent.

She felt the way a Portuguese poet had expressed it – In every corner of my soul there is an altar to a different god.

And the personality that served at one of those altars at any time would dictate her perceptions, beliefs, feelings, words, gestures, facial expressions, body postures, behaviour...

Each personality inside her seemed to have its own style and motivation, completely different from her other 'selves'. And each of these personalities definitely had her own attitude towards life. That was why life sometimes filled her with enthusiasm and all the fun of the fair, but at other times it seemed completely meaningless, a humdrum routine; now an adventure, then a nightmare. Endless variations. Endless transformations.

Adie decided she must actually be a whole crowd of opposing people:

5

intellectual aesthete, common peasant; exemplary wife, nasty bitch; a staid and organised person, a wild party-girl…

They all masqueraded as Adie, an alleged single personality. Each one constantly fought with the others to enjoin their mythology for life, their principles, their desires, their ambitions. And they were sending her crazy!

The phone rang and it was for her.

'Do these people really believe so passionately in the importance of their work?' Adie wondered, while listening to the next 'unbeatable value' offer for advertising services. The caller pressed Adie insistently to meet up for a presentation. Adie struggled, but eventually convinced him that an e-mail would suffice at the moment.

"How can these people take themselves and what they're doing so seriously?" Adie believed in doing her job responsibly, but she didn't have this serious, workaholic attitude, neither did it take her much time or effort. That's why she wondered whether people pretended or whether they really were so busy and had an extraordinary amount of work.

"Perhaps they do believe," Adie decided, feeling superior that she was above all that. Yet she also felt sad that she had failed to develop any comparable dedication to at least one of her numerous involvements. Nothing she did felt sufficiently meaningful to Adie. Nothing was that one thing, her true vocation and purpose in life. Perhaps this was the reason for her failure to achieve any of what society deemed 'success': fame, power and lots of money.

All Adie wanted was the simple house she could not afford to buy, her own cosy, quiet space surrounded by meadows and forest. Though her heart was set on such a house, she was left cold by ideas in the style of so many American self-help books and films (like the movie The Secret), on how to attract whatever you desire. To Adie it all seemed to revolve around obsession with money. 'Spiritual materialism', one of her friends called it.

Money wasn't the thing for Adie. She was missing something much deeper. And despite twenty years of trying on different doctrines, philosophies, religions and practices, she had not found anything that filled her desperate void … until the day she had met Alexey.

She first met Alexey at a seminar he was running, aimed at psychologists. She joined the forum expecting to learn how to apply the techniques of Neuro Linguistic Programming. NLP[1] had become all the rage lately. Adie had read hundreds of impressive testimonials of proven speedy results delivered by its techniques. And it was also justified as a serious science. But, from books alone, Adie was finding it difficult to convert the theory into practical application.

She had entered the seminar with apprehension. Most of the others there seemed to be professionals who knew each other, while she was not even a psychologist. Adie had graduated as a theologian.

Now, twenty years later, she knew she had chosen to study theology because she believed it was the only path that would make her life meaningful. All the usual professions seemed to her somehow superficial: just mindless occupations to pass the years until retirement.

Adie had trusted that theology would offer her something deeply meaningful. What could be deeper than God who is beyond all known frames and limits? But, too soon, she realised she had landed in an institution which, over the centuries, had blocked out God's voice. Everything was geared up to convince her that the life she is living is meaningless; at least it would be until she died.

The phone rang again and this time it was Alexey! They arranged to meet straight after work at Office Two (their name for the cafe around the corner from where the seminar was held) to discuss the project they were working on.

A year had passed by since Adie had introduced herself sheepishly at that seminar, as the theologian who could not find herself, never mind God! On that day, Adie had entered an incredible process she still did not fully understand, but she was relishing watching the increasingly amazing effects of it. To most people, the things Alexey was drawing them into would be considered crazy, but Adie was carried away by them.

It had really all started after the seminar, when the group of eight moved to the nearby pub for a drink. Most engaged in deep discussions of cases from their practices, using language that went over Adie's head and she felt out of place.

Yet, after a glass of wine, she plucked up the courage to turn to Alexey

[1] NLP - Interpersonal communicative model and alternative approach to psychology, invented by Richard Bandler and John Grinder in the 1970s

and ask him the question, which was overwhelming her. She started somewhat evasively, as if she were not talking about herself, but generally:

"Alexey, what would you say to a person who can't find meaning in anything he does, and everything seems insignificant to him?"

"I would say that this person is thinking too much." Adie felt unsure whether Alexey was being serious, or perhaps dismissive. She felt knots being tied in her guts, the way she used to react at exams. Her hands began to sweat and she blushed. Adie drank a long draught of her wine to mask the awkwardness she was sensing. The conversation had already taken another direction, but she resolved to use the occasion and get an answer.

Alexey was sitting next to her. A gentle touch to his arm was enough to gain his attention. "Alexey, I can't find my calling. I have no idea what I should do with my life. I am completely lost. I cannot find the meaning of my existence. I feel so depressed…"

"What do you like to eat the most?" Alexey interrupted. The others were listening now, and they laughed at this. Adie would have felt she was being teased had she not already realised that Alexey was something special, a rare kind of person.

All eyes were upon Adie, awaiting her answer. Someone could not resist offering a hint: "Chocolate!" They all laughed again.

Adie was no longer perturbed. "No. I love chocolate, but most of all I love … cheese … Danish Blue!" She had no idea how this cheese came into her mind, but the thought of it made her saliva ooze. "Mmmm, yummy!" she murmered.

"Phew, yuk!" someone else responded, drawing more laughter.

All immediately fell silent when Alexey began to speak: "Listen to what you should do now. Buy some Danish Blue…"

"I have!" Adie exclaimed.

"Cut one liiiiiittle piece," Alexey continued. "As little as this." He indicated a tiny gap between the tips of his forefinger and thumb, no more than a centimetre. "Put this tiiiiiiny piece of cheese in a biiiiiig plate. Then, take one biiiiiig fork…"

"Could it be the two-pronged fork I use for serving up fish?"

interrupted Adie.

"Perfect!" Alexey assured her. "Take this fork, stick it in the cheese, and eat it with the greatest pleasure."

Everyone laughed, Adie too. Then suddenly her face registered horror: "But my partner at home will think I've gone crazy if he sees me eating cheese like that." She laughed as she pictured the shocked face of her dearest.

"No one needs to see you," said Alexey.

"OK, then!" Adie agreed. She stayed just a few minutes more before making her apologies to leave. She couldn't wait to try out her new alternative. All she could think of was how and when she would do it.

As much as she wanted to, Adie realised there would be no chance to eat her cheese that way tonight. But at least the thought of it perked up her mood for the rest of her evening. She went to bed with a smile and fell asleep immediately.

2. CHAPTER TWO

The next morning, she walked to the kitchen to boil water for the coffee, went to the bathroom and then back to the kitchen. She stopped for a minute in the middle of the room wondering whether to eat the cheese straight away or to drink her coffee first. She decided she wanted to be fully awake for the cheese ritual, so she sat down with her mug.

After her coffee, Adie stood up, went to the kitchen door and listened… nothing. Only she was awake. She retrieved her beloved Danish Blue from the fridge, cut a tiny piece, as directed by Alexey, and placed it at the centre of a large, round serving plate that she chose from the cupboard. Then she unhooked the huge two-pronged fish-fork hanging beside the stove.

Adie listened again at the door. All was still quiet. She seated herself at the kitchen table, the cheese in front of her, her heart quickening. She gripped the big fork, skewered the sliver of cheese on one prong, and guided it carefully to her mouth.

To Adie, this whole performance seemed as amusing as it was ridiculous. She played along with sounds of blissful enjoyment as the bitter creaminess of the cheese melted into the saliva on her tongue. But before she had even swallowed it, she quickly arose, washed the plate and the fork, wiped them dry and put them back in their places, before anyone might discover evidence of her secret.

Adie had not been expecting any answers from performing her ritual. But she was surprised by the growing feeling that followed: a strange enthusiasm, a relieved feeling of liberation.

Now, from her time spent in the company of Alexey, Adie readily recognised that feeling. It came whenever she did things that had no logic, that were so absurd that they blew away the constant inner dialogue that ran amok through her mind.

The ritual she performed that morning was totally different from all the formulas abounding in various books that offered a structured approach to happiness: follow step one, then two, then three to get four.

These formulas only created great expectations that rarely ever became a reality. The task set by Alexey with the cheese ran contrary to that doomed algorithmic approach. Rather, it aimed to destroy the very possibility of anticipation, by taking her out of the framework into which her mind was locked: that Adie lacked a vocation.

Adie turned the radio on. That was her usual habit on entering the kitchen first thing each morning, but today, she had wanted no distraction while eating the cheese. The radio brought the solemn sound of trumpets to Adie's ears. She recognised it immediately: the ever-popular Triumphal March from the opera Aida.

"Hah!" she exclaimed to herself. "Very interesting, indeed!" Though she was fed up with people associating her name with Verdi's Aida, it seemed strange that right now she was hearing exactly this fragment of that opera, after which she was named 'by chance'.

She was named Aida because when her father had proposed to her mother the same march was being played on the radio. Her mother, for some reason, had attributed a special meaning to this fact and when she was told that she had given birth to a girl (about which, who knows how, she had been certain from the moment she found out she was pregnant), she insisted on calling the little girl Aida. Even she could not explain why but she was absolutely sure that this was the right name for her daughter.

Adie, for her part and for reasons she could not explain, had grown up with a deep and sincere conviction that she was exceptional. Around the age of 20, she had firmly believed that her life would be extraordinary (because she would make it so). Then, little by little, she began to doubt it, started getting confused and hesitant until she got completely lost.

At their next meeting Adie asked Alexey whether "her" march playing on the radio, immediately after completing her cheese ritual, might be anything more than a coincidence.

"These things can sometimes pull in strange ways, even quite shocking, and their effects show up in unexpected directions. Personally, I prefer not to believe in coincidences – I find it more interesting," Alexey answered, smiling.

There were three hours remaining to the end of the workday. Adie forced herself to continue processing the monthly sales checks. One by one, she opened the traders' files then she entered the figures in the compendious table, from which the summary data could be followed. She noted with satisfaction a significant and lasting increase in sales for both products she had been focusing on recently.

She had been concentrating on her work and when she glanced at the clock she saw it was time to dash for her meeting with Alexey. She smiled as she thought how they would laugh when she told him about the incident with the old lady that morning. She quickly switched off the computer, wished her colleagues a nice evening and left.

While going through the turnstile, she took a deep breath and with a blissful expression paced along the alley. In this direction it looked different. Or maybe Adie had made herself perceive it so... She called the passage from the bus stop to the office 'leading in', and in the opposite direction 'leading out'. Actually, both of them lead to one and the same place, to some other state of the soul, but in a different way.

A pigeon on the ground sensed her approach, fluttered its wings and flew up in the air just in front of her. Adie sensed the whiff of the wings, even its specific smell and she didn't mind in the slightest.

But six months ago this just could not have happened.

Adie had a phobia of pigeons and though it sounded ridiculous to the others, these birds terrified her. She would even cross the street to avoid them. One evening after a seminar, she was leaving the building a few steps ahead of the group. Opening the door onto the street, she disturbed a group of pigeons. As they fluttered into the air, Adie shrieked and pulled back so quickly she trod on someone's foot. She would have crashed to the ground but for a firm pair of hands that grasped her arms and steadied her.

"What happened, Adie?" Alexey, who was with the group, asked.

"I am very sorry but I am terrified of pigeons." She was still under the effect of her fright; she took the plunge and started apologizing in confusion.

The others' faces expressed compassion, but as to be expected, they were on the verge of laughing when they found out what it was all about.

"Why?" asked Alexey, also smiling, but with a note of concern in his voice.

"I don't know. I have no idea." Adie answered.

"Don't worry! We'll rid you of it." He said.

"How?" Adie exclaimed.

"Here is your task until our next meeting: when you think of pigeons - draw them."

"How should I draw them?" Adie didn't quite understand what exactly was expected from her.

"As you like. And as you can. Just when you happen to think about pigeons - draw pigeons, any way you wish: on canvas, on old newspaper, on the wall... Wherever you want and as much as you want, until you get bored with it," instructed Alexey.

"I can draw only ducks," said Adie. "Daddy taught me a long time ago how to make from the figure of 'two' ducks so that I wouldn't be upset if I get a poor mark[2] at school." The found memory cheered her up and the expression on her face brightened.

"Well, then draw ducks, but you'll know that they are actually pigeons," said Alexey smiling. "Next week you can report back on how you're doing and we'll decide what to do further."

"Fine." Adie accepted the suggestion. She took out of her bag a notebook and a pen and as she was walking, she drew several pigeons and showed the painting to Alexey.

"Is this good?" she asked.
"Excellent." He encouraged her.

___

[2] In Bulgaria 2 is the poorest school grade a child can receive for their work.

Adie diligently drew ducks-pigeons the whole week. And as she did so she felt that her attitude to the birds was shifting. She lived on the top floor of a large townhouse in the city centre and her kitchen window overlooked the rooves of neighbouring buildings. There were always pigeons perched up there. Every time Adie entered the kitchen she would first open the door cautiously and peek to check for a pigeon inside: she was afraid that the window might have been carelessly left open and some bird might have entered.

Her big breakthrough came on the Sunday morning. Adie was in the kitchen having her wake-up coffee, grappling with a fiendish Sudoku puzzle. A pigeon landed right on her window sill. Of course, the window was closed. But even so, if this had happened a week ago, Adie would have leapt from her chair to beat wildly on the window-pane with her newspaper. Before her panic subsided, she would have continued beating until the terrified pigeon was just a small dot, flying away in the distance.

Today, Adie simply leaned over casually from her chair. The window was just within reach of her cautiously outstretched arm. Actually taking care not to scare the bird, she gently tapped her fingers on the pane.

The pigeon cocked its head in her direction, strutted a few tiny steps along the window ledge as it surveyed Adie, then casually stretched its wings and flapped away.

Adie smiled, folded herself back into her chair with smug satisfaction. She returned to pondering her Sudoku, absent-mindedly sketching an extended family of duck-pigeons around the margin.

At her next meeting with Alexey and the group she reported her improvement but confessed she still had her fear of pigeons. Then Alexey suggested she start copying the birds by imitating their fluttering with her arms, with the movements of her body – their movement, to 'coo', to 'pick up crumbs with her peak from the ground' … and anything else she could think of that was characteristic of the pigeons' behaviour.

The people from the group had some fun with this idea and after a few demonstrations, accompanied by loud laughter moved on to the exercises Alexey had prepared for the evening.

Taking her task seriously, the next two-three weeks Adie pretended to be a pigeion, whenever she remembered to do so and had the opportunity to be on her own. In the beginning she was looking for such opportunities, then – only when she remembered to do so, more and more rarely, while at one moment she forgot about it.

She found out that she had been cured from her phobia when one day, engrossed in her thoughts, while passing a shopfront, she heard the flap of wings. She sensed movement in the air and then realised she had passed without as much as a flinch through a group of a dozen pigeons, gathered there for a feast.

The bus came almost immediately and Adie arrived at the meeting point 10 minutes early. Alexey was already there – in the company of two women and, as usual, he was drinking beer and lighting up one cigarette after another. Adie sat at a nearby table and after a while he joined her.

"You won't believe it." Alexey said, while they were still shaking hands.

"What is it?" Adie encouraged him to continue.

"These two women are my colleagues, you may recall that one of them attended a seminar once?" he added.

"Yes, I remember, it was about a month ago" Adie confirmed.

"Right," Alexey said and continued, "Then, after the seminar, we were sitting again here and she complained that she and her husband had been trying to adopt a child and there was always some obstacle or other. She had become desperate; she was almost ready to pay somebody under the table to pull some strings. She asked me that day if I could do some magic and help her. I assured her I could, but of course we were only joking. To laugh is just about the only thing you can do in a situation like that. And that was all we did.

"But yesterday, she called me on the phone, all emotional, and she told me that after we had talked that day things had started to happen. And now they have a child! And … you will never guess … the boy is called Alex!"

"Come on…" Adie exclaimed.

"Yes! And we haven't done anything. You can hardly say that we've done anything special …We just made it into a joke, but obviously that was enough to ease the tension and to let things happen – and very quickly"

Alexey said, smiling: 'The Universe decided to make me a Godfather.' "

"I'm speechless…" was the only comment Adie could make.

At that moment she had a slightly gormless expression on her face, not sure what to make of the story. On one hand, from personal experience, she was sure that sometimes things worked out in exactly this way. But then again, she continued doubting that such seemingly 'insignificant' 'interventions" could bring about such dramatic changes.

Her way of thinking had been programmed to follow certain patterns and algorithms, which were easy to understand: if there is a result, the algorithm works, and if there isn't - the algorithm doesn't work. And both success and failure can always be measured. But here Adie has to deal with something quite different. There was no algorithm to trace – there was just development of potential and that could become everything.

Alexey, his two colleagues, Adie … every person, in fact … was a developer of the same universal potential, available to all. Anyone could manifest it through themselves in whatever situation they chose. But hardly anyone knew how. That's why, to most people, such incidents appeared to be, and were usually explained as, simply serendipity.

They remained silent for a while, then noticed it was time to make their way to the seminar. On the way Adie told Alexey the story of the old woman she had tamed on the bus that morning. He laughed a lot.

Alexey then recalled a similar incident. An old woman had started nagging him, claiming he had pushed ahead of her in what she claimed was a queue. Instead of arguing, Alexey mentally presented her with a juicy apple as a gift, and she soon quietly relaxed. This evoked new laughter, along with jokes about how easy it was to placate bad-tempered old women in this way.

Cheered up, they went upstairs in the office where the others had already gathered. In a great mood, Alexey began by sharing his colleagues's good news of her new child. He followed up with two similar stories, of 'magic' that had surprised even him with their unexpected outcomes. Both were from what Alexey called 'friend sessions', where he always tried unconventional ways to help solve the problems.

The first story was that of a friend who had a common problem – he wanted some work done on his house, but could not afford even the cheapest quote. The two of them were in a bar and when Alexey heard the problem he asked his friend if there was something very ordinary he had never done at home.

The man confessed he had never watered the flowers. Alexey pointed to some plants there in the bar. "Go get some water and water those!" The bar was crowded but this friend was a good sport and enjoyed a laugh. So he asked the barmaid for a jug of water then squeezed past bewildered customers to give a drink to all the flowers in the room.

While this craziness had them both laughing, Alexey urged his friend to ring the builder and ask for a discount. The call got straight through to the boss of the building firm. The brief exchange left Alexey's friend dumbstruck.

When he finally managed to say something, it was Alexey's turn to drop his jaw, speechless. It appeared that at just that moment the manager was celebrating her birthday and obviously she was in such a great mood that she told him they were going to do the work on his house for free, as a present… like that…

The second friend was having unexpected problems arranging a mortgage. All had been going well, then suddenly the bank said there was a problem and the procedure was stopped. It was more than worrying: she'd already put down a deposit on the house and desperately needed that mortgage.

Alexey told her to picture in her mind something unusual that she particularly liked. After some deep thought, she said, "Amphora".

Just at that moment, Alexey's phone rang and he went outside to speak. When he came back after a minute, he saw the woman standing petrified, eyes popping out, staring at the television. She just about managed to point at the television screen and when he looked he saw that there was a report about some excavations and the unique archeological finds discovered there, among which there was … an amphora.

When she came to her senses the woman told him that the amphora she saw on the television was almost identical to the one she had imagined a few minutes ago. "So, you've hit the right image." Alexey said and suggested she should call her bank in the morning.

The next morning, Alexey's friend called him. The bank had actually called her, to apologise for some misunderstanding. She did not understand what had happened, but the mortgage was approved.

All listened with expressions which seemed to show both amazement and disbelief. Then they started a lively discussion, but as they didn't know what exactly to say or what exactly to think, their comments were directed towards Alexey's abilities to do 'miracles'. Alexey objected he was not telling these stories to claim he was a magician but to highlight what can happen when we act from a position contrary to structured linear thinking. He asked them to open their notebooks and divide a page down the middle. Then Alexey dictated what to put in each column.

On the left side: Established logic, linear processes:

- corresponds to the consecutive order of things;
- actions are based on logical grounding;
- skills for planning and active realization of the plan;
- searching for logical connections;
- intellectual thinking and reasoning;
- working out of the details;
- state of definiteness;
- consecutive going through the variants in searching for the right decision.

On the right: Beyond the logic, non-linear processes:

- correspond to the state of superposition, to the whole space and beyond it;
- spontaneous and intuitive actions;
- following inner movement and trust in life;
- absence of obvious connection between the reason and consequence;
- sensual and emotional perception;
- fully, holistic perception of the world;
- state of indefiniteness, unpredictable future;
- holistic view and finding the necessary option right away.

Alexey told them to think about the management of reality according to the two approaches and next time share their thoughts what could be expected if we accepted each of them.

With this the meeting was over and Adie headed quickly towards the bus stop so that she could be home as quickly as possible. Two buses passed by while she was walking… she would have to wait. Unless … "I wish you a cheerful mood and I am giving it to you in the shape of a big cold rakiya[3]" – She directed mentally towards some imaginary driver. In less than a minute she saw the headlights of a bus coming from the end of the street. When it approached she noticed that there was a second one coming just a little distance behind.

"Wow!" marvelled Adie. "These guys sure are thirsty!" she laughed, "Well, I'm feeling generous. I'll treat you both to a beer!" Adie continued teasing the drivers mentally while she was getting on board.

---

[3] Rakiya is an alcoholic beverage that is produced by distillation of fermented fruit; it is a popular beverage in Bulgaria and throughout the Balkans.

3. CHAPTER THREE

The next morning Adie got up again in her "shitty" mood. This time, however, there was a reason: her loved one's awful snoring. Adie had never heard such a loud snore. Her partner had not snored recently (or at least she hadn't heard him), but she had an idea what might have been going on last night to revive his habit.

"You'll get what you deserve, bitch!" Adie threatened, forcing her tired body out of bed. She was sure the blame lay with the new doctor who'd replaced the old 'snorologist' that Adie had let go.

Although this story ran like a legend among her colleagues from the seminars, this morning Adie didn't feel like laughing at all.

It didn't take Adie much effort to get into the spirit of what Alexey was showing. After the story with the cheese and some similar "performances" Adie herself started generating 'wild ideas' quite easily. Her first success was that she had succeeded in stopping her beloved's snoring.

Actually, Adie couldn't work out if he had suddenly stopped snoring or she had just stopped hearing him, but she didn't care. The only thing that she cared about was the result, namely the fact that after months of waking at night and quarrelling in the morning, she could again sleep peacefully and without waking up all night.

The idea struck her after a seminar at which Alexey told how he 'murmured' a new job for the wife of one of his friends. The woman had been searching months for a job, without even landing an interview for herself.

One night Alexey had been visiting them and they complained to him about the situation and, instead of expressing compassion and giving them some standard useless advice, he convinced them to try something different. He made the woman develop the darkest scenario possible by hyperbolizing the problem. She described it with his help – she loses all her money, her house and remains in the street, then she saw herself dressed in a shabby coat and how a stray dog was trying to take from her a hunk of stale bread.

The whole time they laughed a lot and to make it even crazier her husband 'played' the Marseillaise on a comb. Then Alexey told the woman to make a little person out of plasticine. She did so with a lump of her child's. She even put on it wings, so that it could be quicker, as the task of the fellow-assistant was to go and "murmur" to the potential employers to hire her. They laughed a lot on the folly they were making and decided to finish with a beer. The husband turned the radio on and at this moment all were aghast: the tune playing was La Marseillaise.

That had all happened less than a month ago. Today Alexey's friends had called him: his wife had found a very good job, and well paid. They were inviting Alexey round to celebrate with another beer … and to sing La Marseillaise.

Adie was extraordinarily impressed with this story and decided to try something similar to cope with her beloved's snoring, which at the moment was just as important as finding of her vocation.

She started imagining what would happen if he didn't stop snoring. She saw herself woken up in the middle of the night by his snoring. In despair she reached for Dostoevsky's Brothers Karamazov and in a moment the fat volume has landed on her partner's head.

He grumbled - just once and then subsided. She started pulling him, but he didn't budge; then she switched on the lamp and saw that she had crushed his head; then, she phoned the police and gave herself up, the court proclaimed her crazy and sent her to an asylum, where she spent the rest of her life, swaying in a rocking chair, dirty, disheveled and snoring.

Here the scenario ended – Adie had exhausted it. She sensed that she felt like crying. Then she realized that this was just a grotesque story. Again she replayed the scenario in her mind and this time the absurdity of some of the scenes made her laugh. She even felt snobbish satisfaction in being such a refined murderess with the fact that she used as s weapon one truly genius literary work as Karamasov's Brothers.

Then she decided that she should reinforce her scenario with an image. She remembered that her boyfriend loved cats very much and she made a drawing of a cute kitten sleeping peacefully. She slipped this under his pillow and went to sleep full of hope. But it didn't work. The snoring seemed to be lighter than usual, but the result was not satisfactory enough. She was on the verge of giving up on Alexey's nonsense ideas, when it struck her that there was no way the kitten would work. 'How can you be so stupid, Adie?' yelled Adie to herself.

'Of course, they would purr and snore all night. The sweeter the kitten purred, the sweeter he would snore!' She thought a bit and came to the conclusion that her beloved was quite a conventional and reasonable person, who respected science and medicine, and he even had experience in this field. So she decided to try with a doctor. This was more complicated but she somehow managed with the drawing.

The result was very good – the doctor seemed competent and experienced. Adie took out the kitten and put the doctor in its place under the pillow. She had also provided him with an injection in his hand for emergency and before she went to bed she ordered him to look after her dear during the night.

This night Adie slept without waking and when she realized this in the morning she couldn't believe it. Of course, she decided that it might be an accident. She could hardly wait until the next evening, and the next, and the next … 'The miracle' continued for months right up until the present…

In the beginning her partner looked at her inquisitively, when every night before she went to bed, she lift the pillow and instructed the doctor beneath to take good care of him. He shook his head and commented invariably:

"You've gone totally nuts with these seminars!"

Yet he had to admit that something unusual was happening – Adie didn't push him at night to shake him when his snoring had woken her up. And soon he even started reminding her in the evening: "Did you tell the doctor?"

After some time the piece of paper on which she had drawn the doctor got crushed, it started tearing and she decided to send the "old" doctor to retire and to appoint a younger doctor to the post. She wrote a thank-you letter to the old doctor 'Snore', wished him good health, a long and happy life and she was about to begin drawing his substitute when her dear came in. He asked her what she was doing and she explained that his snoring would be taken care of by a new doctor.

"Couldn't it be a young female doctor?" her friend asked.

Adie's hand froze over the page. She answered reluctantly, through clenched teeth, "Sure. Why not?"

Adie knew these snorologists' interventions were nothing but a parody, yet she could hardly contain the jealousy she felt. She finished the picture of the new doctor ... female ... and instantly regretted that she had made her look so good.

In the evening, as usual, she lifted the pillow and ordered the doctor to look after her dear one during the night. Just as she was kneeling on the bed in her pyjamas, her beloved tickled her bare feet – something that drove Adie mad. She jumped up, turned instantly and, still holding the pillow upwards, she hissed something angrily at him. Then she dropped the pillow and went to sleep.

4. CHAPTER FOUR

That night she woke up from a snoring which would have risen the dead. She had never heard anything like it and she didn't believe that her beloved could make sounds like that. She elbowed him roughly. He rolled over and continued sleeping quietly. Adie, however, was now fully awake. In her thoughts she replayed the scene when she ordered the young female doctor to look after her man during the night... and she realised that the medical woman must have seen how Adie reacted to the tickling.

"Well, well," Adie said to herself, I can't expect much good from those two." She tossed and turned in her bed for a long time, fell asleep at dawn and could hardly get up when she heard the alarm. Her usual morning coffee almost made her throw up, which always happened when she had not slept enough. She somehow completed her morning routine, dressed, and went to work.

When she reached the alley, she felt better. She walked quite slowly, taking in lungfulls of fresh air, affirming to herself that she was breathing in energy and joy. She exhaled slowly, pushing firmly from her diaphragm, imagining a powerful piston clearing out her fatigue and her cranky mood. It made her feel dizzy, but she also felt much better.

She somehow managed to grit her teeth and get through her day in the office, but instead of going straight home after work, on the way back she stopped at the post office. Adie resolutely went in, approached the counter and bought a pre-paid envelope for a letter abroad. At home, she took the envelope from her bag, tore out a sheet of paper from a notebook, sat at the table and started writing in English:

To whom it may concern:
Dear Sir or Madam,
This letter heartily recommends Dr. Snore as a highly qualified snorologist and the best candidate you may ever have for the vacant PhD specialisation in your Snorology Department. I am confident that the experience of Dr. Snore will contribute significantly to the future development of scientific studies on the snoring process in humans.
Sincerely yours,
Aida

Adie went to her bedroom and retrieved the drawing of the medical woman from under her partner's pillow. The lady doctor went into the envelope with the letter and Adie sealed it. Then she pulled a piece of paper from her pocket, unfolded it, and copied from it the following address on the envelope:

Harvard Medical School
260 Longwood Avenue
Boston, MA 02115
USA

Adie put the envelope in her handbag, changed out of her work clothes, and cooked dinner, shortly before her dearest came home. He helped her with the salad, they ate and the evening took its normal course.

Later, when Adie was preparing to go to sleep and lifted the pillow to give instructions to the doctor beneath, her beloved peeked to see his young female doctor. To his surprise she wasn't there. A young male doctor was there instead.

"Where is my lady-doctor?" he asked.

"She received an invitation to specialize on Snorology in Harvard and she accepted." Adie explained and added. "I even gave her a letter of recommendation."

He laughed in disbelief – obviously Adie was joking. She shrugged and said:

"I am sorry, but nobody would refuse to go to Harvard even for you."

"And where is she now?" her beloved asked again.

"On the plane, I suppose" Adie responded quite seriously.

Her beloved looked at her silently. His expression, though, was saying: 'Right, you are crazy, but that doesn't mean I have to go crazy too...' Adie held his gaze stoically. She'd already had a hearty laugh while writing the letter and put it with the young lady-doctor into an envelope addressed to Harvard.

She'd nearly split her sides at the thought of some academic at Harvard opening the envelope to find a drawing of a woman doctor and a crazy letter of recommendation for her as a highly qualified snorologist who would specialise there.

"Sorry if you're disappointed, but that's the way it is," smiled Adie.

Overcome by the exhaustion of her previous sleepless night, she fell asleep as soon as her head hit the pillow.

5. CHAPTER FIVE

The next morning Adie noted that the new doctor was doing a great job. On her way to work she dropped the letter to Harvard into a mailbox.

Her time at work flew as she had several meetings which had filled her day. She felt a little tired but when she left the office she cheered up. She turned on her player to listen to "Victory", her favourite tune by the Bond string quartet. It always filled Adie with a strong feeling of élan, so powerful that it moved her to tears and she liked it very much. It was an ambivalent emotion, sad and happy at the same time and quite real – just what Adie was feeling inside. She didn't care at all that some 'connoisseurs' consider Bond the "trash" of classical music.

Adie's father was a musician. She had grown up surrounded by his fellow musicians - players of just about every instrument: drums, guitar, clarinet, gadulka, tambourine[4] ... Whenever those musicians leapt up on the stage in the restaurants where they performed, she always felt as if they were playing especially for her. So she always listened to them carefully. Sometimes she would gleefully clap her little hands. Other times she might sob tears, unable to explain why.

From an early age, music had been very personal to Adie, and still remained deeply associated with her emotions. Her mp3 player was full of every imaginable style of music, as long as it had spoken to her soul at some time in some way. She could not live without it.

Her personal stereo was the first and only thing she had ever asked her

---

[4] Gadulka and tambourine are typical Bulgarian folk music instruments.

parents to buy her. At the time a Walkman was the latest device, newly launched, and Adie was set on owning one. But, being the latest thing, they were also expensive, and Adie's family was by no means well-off. She endured a long and deep inner struggle before she could bring herself to ask for the money. Her parents bought her the Walkman immediately, without a fuss, but Adie still suffered pangs of guilt about the hardship her teenage fad may have caused them.

Adie couldn't wait to tell Alexey about the unexpected twist to the snoring story. She was sure the others in the group would also be highly amused, but she would bet that none of the practitioners among them would ever suggest something like that to their clients as a therapy.

The practitioners were finding it especially difficult to fathom Alexey's approach. During all their years of academic study, they had been drilled into making diagnoses. They were taught they must dig deep into problems and seek reasons, causes and explanations based on accepted theories. They were taught to apply tests to their clients (who they even referred to as patients) to measure the parameters of their personalities. Maybe then, after all that, they could try to figure out some solution to the problem.

And so they went on, even though in most cases this approach simply did not work. They had become lost in their own tangled attempts to interpret unique experiences according to the generalised models put forward by accepted authorities. Often, in trying to lead a client out of one perceived dysfunctional pattern of behaviour or perception, they actually led them into just another equally dysfunctional model.

The psychologists in the group were always seeking explanations, just as they were trained to do. Alexey was trying to convince them this was not necessary. They always wanted him to describe step by step procedures, to give them another theory to explain it all. But Alexey always asserted that there was no theory for his approach. If he created one, it would probably stop working.

He explained that modern civilisation was suffering from what he called *a verbal and intellectual obesity*. All the time, there were people giving explanations, yet almost never did anyone offer specific actions to resolve a situation. He called it a harmful passion for explanations. This was harming people directly because they accepted the explanation as the truth, leaving themselves open to all kinds of manipulations hidden within those explanations.

To illustrate his words, he told them a joke, which Adie found particularly amusing:

"Two doctors were walking down a hospital corridor. Hobbling towards them, they saw a man bent double, barely able to walk.

"Polio," one of the doctors announced to the other, "This is polio."

"No," judged the second doctor, "It is surely a case of advanced arthritis."

While they argued, the man approached them and asked in a tortured voice: "Excuse me. Do you know where the toilet is?"

Alexey taught them to seek less explanation. Instead, he encouraged them to direct their attention to what is happening, and seek to clarify what it is we are doing that makes it happen.

He told them that many clients had actually learned from their psychologists and psychiatrists enviable skill in explaining their problems, then simply used these explanations to find excuses that served their own advantage. No real solution to any problem had been found; they had not moved even one iota away from the problem.

The countless anti-stress programs provided a good example. The basic idea of these was to teach people how to relax. "Why don't we instead," asked Alexey, "teach people how not to get stressed in the first place?" He went on with clear passion for what he was saying, "They get stressed, we relax them; they get stressed, we relax them... endlessly!"

"Actually, people do know this deep within themselves," Alexey maintained. "What we need is a way for them to wake up to what they already know. We must find a way out of this problem-sustaining logic that is hammered into our heads from our birth onwards."

What particularly appealed to Adie was something on which Alexey put a special emphasis, namely, that they should approach problematic situations by withdrawing all seriousness from it.

"Seriousness is an extremely dangerous thing," Alexey had once told them. "Have you heard the saying, Serious as a heart attack?" he asked. "Serious people get heart attacks. Seriously. They are forcing the potential to create hindrances for them. And not just inside them. Their internal obstructions start to spill out and produce hindrance events in their external reality. This seriousness is a heavy, rigid, obstructive attitude towards life.

This seriousness is the most serious obstacle to revealing the potential," Alexey concluded.

Adie wrote down those words. To her, they rocked. She realised that in recent years she had taken herself and her life very seriously. So seriously that her jaws ached from constant clenching of her teeth. Yet despite all her serious efforts to find happiness and meaning in her life, Adie felt miserable, lost, insignificant. She felt swamped by stupid problems that seemed to gush out of a huge hole in her life.

Intuitively, she felt there must be a better way of living but she felt helpless to find it alone, she was so badly stuck in the pattern of serious Adie. Like Baron Munchausen, her quest seemed as impossible as having to grasp her own hair to pull herself out of the swamp. Her entire energy was "gone in the windings", as Alexey had rather curiously told her later that day.

Adie and Alexey met in "Office 2" before the seminar, as had become their routine. They began to talk about 'the potential' and how people don't let it flow naturally in their own lives. Adie had been relating the latest in her saga of the 'snorologist', ending by lamenting, "I do not understand what's going on. It's as if one part of my life is happening in a parallel reality outside this one, but it can sometimes materialise in this one, if I let it…"

"If you let it! You see? I couldn't have put it better myself!" Alexey exclaimed, pulling out from his backpack a pen and a roll of sticky tape. He tore off a piece of tape about 20 cm in length, handed it and the pen to Adie, and told her to coil the tape around the pen every time he made a sign to her.

"First model: real - unreal," said Alexey and gave a sign.

Adie wound the tape around the pen once.

"Second model: possible – impossible"

Adie carried out a second winding.

"Third model: what depends on me and what does not depend on me." The tape was wound round the pen a third time.

"These are the basic models that we learn as social beings and accept as guiding principles in our lives," explained Alexey. "The social environment that creates the models that I call for short 'the socium', told you what is real and what is unreal, what is possible and what is impossible, what depends on you and what does not; and you have accepted this as the truth. On top of that, you have created your own additional restrictive definitions and labels, both positive and negative and all the tape in the world would not be enough for them!"

Alexey smiled and paused to stub out his cigarette. He lit another and continued: "The pen is a metaphor of your basic connection with the potential of life. This is your energy. But where does this energy go when you start winding tape around it?" he asked.

Adie screw up her eyes, in thought. "In the winding round the pen?" she offered timidly, hoping for confirmation.

"Exactly! – It soon came - All our energy goes into the winding, thus weakening our connection with the potential."

"Is this why we do not always achieve what we want to do, to be or to have?" Adie probed further.

Alexey drew on his cigarette. "In general, when acting from the position of the personality formed by the socium, according to those three models and our own additions, our efforts to achieve things become very difficult. That's why we are constantly told that life is a struggle, that we must fight with clenched teeth.

Some such crazy philosophy of survival is being fed to us all the time. The great pity is that even after someone has fought, say twenty years, with clenched teeth and got the thing they were fighting for, in most cases they find that it's nothing: it hasn't brought them the happiness they were expecting," Alexey concluded.

"Well, not always true," Adie pointed out. "There have been many examples of people who seem to have achieved exactly what they wanted, and sometimes with great ease."

"Yes," agreed Alexey. "Some really get what they wanted. But I don't know anybody who is happy in all aspects of their lives. Those who have succeeded in one aspect but failed in another, maybe they invented the saying: There is no complete happiness, to justify their failure and find comfort."

"But why," asked Adie, "having succeeded in one area, did they not use the same model to succeed in other aspects of their life?"".

"Because there is no model… no algorithm. In fact, there aren't even any different aspects of life. There are only actions. Either from the position of the personality formed by the socium and transformed into a mini-socium or there are actions beyond that position, from the super-position."

Alexey was now in full flow. "Life is not many-sided. We just think it is, because we act from the position of our mini-socium. Really, there is only one universal potential that each of us can reveal. We do not own it. We do not even carry it. We are just the developers of this potential.

"If our connection with it were not weakened because all our energy has gone into the winding, we would probably be able to do everything we wanted, and with great ease. It would reflect in our life as one integral whole, as it was originally at our birth.

"Different pieces of our lives are artificially created. Our lives have been broken into work, love, money, free time and countless other life-piece fabrications for which thousands of foolish self-help guides have been composed: How to build a successful career, How to create ideal relationships, How to be wealthy…

"However, if we learn how to live from the super-position instead of the mini-socium, then there will be no need to fight on a thousand fronts, nor even on one. We won't fight at all. We'll live our lives quite differently, in its original completeness and full value.

"To come back to your question about why we succeed only sometimes, only to a certain extent, only in some aspect… When we do succeed, it's only when one of our 'windings' has loosened. That's what happens with people who manage to do things with ease, as you say. At some point some winding has loosened, and this allows them to connect to the potential. Do you see." Alexey concluded with confidence.

Adie, however, continued to harass him with her questions. "When and how do the windings loosen?"

"Let me pee and get a beer" Alexey smiled as he stood.

Adie was resting her elbow on the table, absentmindedly coiling a lock of hair around her finger as she always did when she was thinking intensively. She was startled by Alexey's return.

"I think I have an explanation," she claimed before he was even seated again.

"About what?" Alexey asked.

"About the windings, when and how they loosen." Adie answered.

"Curious to hear it," Alexey encouraged.

"I was thinking. Despite all these models, restrictions, obligations, requirements, rules and so on that the socium imposes, not all of us are totally crazy yet. I don't think I am. It's true that my life is not what would make me happy but it's not an absolute disaster, some nice things happen too …" Adie paused as if she was mentally scrolling through a movie of these good things.

"And?" Alexey invited her to continue.

"I think I am not mad and have not yet committed suicide because somehow, intuitively, I managed to loosen the windings whenever they tightened too much. For example, I'd watch a comedy and laugh, or I'd ride my bicycle for hours… go for coffee with a friend, or cry. These things help to loosen the grip of the windings," Adie reasoned.

"Imagine then," Alexey prompted, "what it would be like to be able to loosen the windings consciously, even completely get rid of them. That's where the seminars are leading us. I too am still a beginner in this process, and even I feel constantly surprised by the things that happen when we act from the super-position… from beyond the position of the personality and the socium."

"That is why I share all these exercises, to help us escape the position of the socium, small and large. I'm convinced it will be useful for the therapists in the group. When they work with their clients in therapy, if they do not escape that position, what happens is that two small sociums crash into a large one, and the results won't be good." Alexey looked on with his typical gentle smile.

Adie said nothing. She was wondering how those ideas came to Alexey's, and why she hadn't thought of them. She felt somewhat foolish, as she always did whenever she met someone smarter than herself. Meaning someone who was able to impress and provoke her intellect, which did not happen often.

Alexey broke the silence. "For today I have prepared something to do with this, which you'll find very interesting," he glanced at his watch, "and it's time to go."

Both stood and Alexey returned his pen and his sticky tape to his bag. As they walked to the seminar, Adie quizzed him, "What else is in this backpack of yours?" She meant that not many people carry around a roll of sticky tape.

Alexey understood her point and laughed, "One never knows what resources one may need!"

Adie smiled and, putting on a wise voice, said: "Yes, sticky tape is an essential resource for connecting with the potential."

"Actually, it's the lack of tape that's needed," Alexey corrected. "But alas, the human brain cannot think of something without thinking of it."

"What do you mean?" Adie asked.

"Do not think of an orange squirrel!" Alexey commanded. "Now, what was the first thing you thought of?"

"Orange squirrel!" Adie laughed.

The two of them slipped into the entrance of the office building where seminar was.

Almost everyone from the group was already there. They greeted each other warmly; they were becoming quite close.

"Let's make a start, as I've prepared something very interesting for today," interrupted Alexey.

They all sat down and, without further delay, Alexey thrust his hand into his bag and pulled out two packs of paper handkerchiefs. The whole group burst into laughter and the jokes started rolling.

"But we don't have runny noses!" protested one.
"No, he uses them in the toilet…" suggested another.

"Are they scented, Alexey?" a third inquired.

Alexey was also laughing. "Sorry, but the last time we met I forgot to ask you to bring handkerchiefs for today's seminar. So, I have improvised." He managed to raise his voice above the others. "Today we will work with the veils," he announced and the voices hushed at once. Now everybody was waiting eagerly for what was to come next.

Alexey began. "We have mentioned the zero-state before. If you recall, this is a concept of quantum physics. It denotes that state of the micro-components when they are neither waves nor particles. They seem to disappear, but actually they are in the zero-state, from which they may appear again as either particles or waves.

"The zero-state is also that state of the whole system in which it cannot be split into separate or independent parts, when it is one whole thing. From this state, any impact from any particular direction creates a new state for that system, a state that has nothing to do with the previous one," Alexey remained silent for a while. All eyes were on him.

He continued. "Actually, this is peculiar to not just elementary particles. Any part of reality, including the mind, may fall or be induced into the zero-state. In this condition, all links and interactions that create the reality for that subject, with all of its inherent properties, are broken. The zero-state is actually a super-position from which any other position can be selected."

Alexey paused again, his eyes scanning their faces. As they were all listening carefully, he continued.

"In the context of our work, in order to emerge from a certain model we must first pass into the neutral state of this super-position. From there, we may choose and then manifest the new reality that we want to have, and in which we will act according to completely different principles and relationships. Now, there are many ways to do this. Alexey paused again. Today, we shall test the method of the veil." Alexey paused again.

The group exchanged glances that said, "Sounds interesting!"

Alexey continued. "This method uses veils of two types: a quantum confusion veil, and a desired state veil.

"The first veil, the quantum confusion one, sets the object that it covers in a purely neutral position. This provides the freedom required for the shift towards another desired state. It separates the object from its interactions with the surrounding environment, and brings it to a level of no-form, no-image, no-feeling. It's called an invisible cover. Through it, the object is brought from a position that was clearly determined to a new position that is indeterminate and contains the active potencies of all available states for that object."

"What?" asked someone "Say that again ..."

Alexey explained. "The zero-state incorporates countless active potentials that are available to the object as a choice for some new, future state."

"Aha…" nodded the man, picking up the thread of Alexey's explanation again.

Alexey continued. "The second type of veil, the desired-state veil, creates the target state from the indeterminate state. This is made possible by conscious use," he stressed the word conscious, "of a technique to create interactions between the zero-state and the desired-state. The interactions could be images, phrases, feelings… anything from the desired future that ensures an intense interaction between the object and the desired state." He paused, "Is everything clear up to here?"

"Yes," the group answered unanimously.

"Now, let's see how the technique works in practice. All you need do is first cover the object with the invisible veil; put over that the desired-state veil, and then carefully remove the first veil. The zero-state veil allows the object to enter the vacuity between all states, which is determined by nothing. It can then be transformed into any desired state.

Alexey stopped to make sure that all were following his instructions, then continued to explain. "Any desire to change a state without passing through the vacuity is like the desire to wear another coat without first removing the coat we already have on. In other words, you must first terminate interactions with all the old rules and connections, by getting into the super-positional state."

Alexey stopped, waiting for a few people who were still writing down his words in their notebooks. "Now leave your notebooks and pens to one side and let's try the technique!"

Alexey opened a pack of tissues and distributed two each. He told the participants to mark one to represent the zero-state veil.

Then he gave instructions on how to place the first veil on their heads and what to do to enter the zero-state. Once in this state, they should call to mind a target state: either an intended future state, or a situation from the past, which could be positively developed into the future.

When they were clear about their desired state, they had to put the second veil over the first, then slowly pull away the first. With their heads covered only by the second veil, they then had to abandon themselves to whatever sensations or images came to them, for however long they lasted.

After the exercise, Alexey, as usual, asked each in turn what they had experienced. Adie was one of the first ones to share. "How it was for you, Adie?" he asked.

"Well, really quite interesting! There was nothing when I looked into my past, but when I thought about the future, I felt something strong pulling me and... well, I really wanted to see what my vocation is in life!"

She smiled and waited for her colleagues' inevitable laughter. Sure enough, they weren't slow off the mark "Ah, Adie, Adie! This vocation of yours will kill you!" someone called out amid much grinning and chuckling.

"And?" Alexey cut short any further comments.

"I was walking along a forest path. It was very beautiful. Out of nowhere, stairs appeared before me; concrete stairs without handrails... like in a new building that hasn't been completed. Well, I climbed up to the top."

"And what did you see from there?" asked Alexey.

"Oh, it's like... someone's tricking me!" Adie said, her voice faltering. "I saw nothing. Absolutely nothing...it wasn't even black. Not normal nothing; it was absolute nothing. I could feel it, rather than see it," Adie finished.

"Well, we shall see what transpires," Alexey simply shrugged, and continued asking the others.

Adie was too absorbed by her own experience to listen to the others.

After the seminar she hurried to her bus stop, feeling unsettled. She waited, deep in confused thought, oblivious to when the next bus might come.

Nearby, three young women were in animated conversation. Adie tried to get what they were saying. She could hear the intonation of their voices, but no clear words, just a background sound among all the other noise of the street. She abandoned her eavesdropping and sank again into her thoughts about the conversation with Alexey before the seminar, about the veils exercise, about the experience that it had brought her...

Suddenly, Adie heard quite clearly: "Have you heard about the stairs?" Adie didn't pay attention. After a while, she heard again, this time even more loudly and clearly: "Do you want a story of the stairs?" And again, "Do you want the tale of the stairs?"

The voice became more insistent each time, until Adie's attention was gripped: "What? Stairs? The tale of the stairs?"

She looked at the girls who continued talking just as animatedly as they were before. She was sure that one of them had said the thing about the stairs. The three girls burst out laughing. Adie pricked up her ears, but the conversation had again turned into an indistinct noise.

"What's going on?" She was startled. It seemed quite odd to hear this talk about stairs right after experiencing her vision at the seminar. It was as if someone had decided that she had to hear only those words and was deliberately drowning out the rest...

"The tale of the stairs ..." Adie repeated to herself silently, as if trying to remember something. Then it came to her: "The Tale of the Stairs! There's a story called "The Tale of the Stairs" by ... who had written it? Was it ... Smirnenski[5]? Yes, Smirnenski! What's it about?" She couldn't remember. "Perhaps that is why I saw nothing from the top of those stairs. The answer must be in The Tale of the Stairs!" These thoughts jostled in Adie's head on the bus home. She couldn't remember the bus coming, nor how she had got on and off, she was so bowled over by what was happening. Still on autopilot, she quickly marched up to the entrance of her apartment block and climbed to the sixth floor, taking two steps at a time. She rang the

[5] Hristo Smirnenski (1989 – 1923) was a Bulgarian proletarian poet and prose writer, known for his moving presentation of the lives of the working class and the poor people.

doorbell and when her beloved opened the door, she kissed him hurriedly, kicked off her shoes and darted inside, explaining, "I need to check something right now. It's very important!"

She sat at the computer still wearing her coat and hat as she searched for "The Tale of the Stairs". Immediately she found the entire tale published online. Adie began reading:

"Who are you?" The Devil asked him…

"I am a plebian by birth and all ragged fellows are my brothers. Oh, so ugly is the earth and so unhappy are the people!"

"What's that supposed to mean?" Adie asked herself. But she continued:

A youth with head raised and clenched fists was saying this. He was standing in front of a staircase – a high staircase of white marble with streaks of pink. He was staring into the distance, where grey mobs of miserable people were massing like the muddled waves of an overflowing river. They stirred, boiled up instantly and raised a forest of dry black arms. A thunder of discontent and ferocious cries shook the air and the echo died down slowly and triumphantly like a distant gunshot.

The mobs grew, they were coming in clouds of yellow dust, separate silhouettes became more and more clearly outlined against the grey background. An old man approached, bent almost to the ground as if he was searching for his youth. A barefoot little girl was holding him by his robe and was looking at the high staircase with her kind eyes, blue as cornflower. She was looking and smiling. Some grey, lean figures in tatters followed, singing a drawling funeral song. Someone was whistling sharply, another, hands thrust in his pockets, was laughing loudly, hoarsely. There was madness burning in his eyes …

"No wonder I don't remember this, it's disgusting!" Adie thought. Reading it made her feel uncomfortable, scared even.

The story recounted how the young man started to climb the stairs to take revenge on the princes and rulers who were responsible for all this suffering of his brethren. But the devil, who guarded the stairs, stopped the young man at each step and demanded a ransom to let him continue. To reach the oppressors, the young man had to hand over his ears, eyes, mind and heart.

The story ended like this:
He had come to the top at last. Suddenly a smile beamed on his face, his eyes started sparkling in quiet joy and his fists relaxed. He looked at the feasting princes, looked

down where the grey tattered mob was roaring and cursing. He looked, but not one of the muscles of his face flinched: it was joyful, beaming, satisfied. All he could see were clothed groups of people whose moans had turned into hymns.

"Who are you?" the Devil asked him in a hoarse, cunning voice.

"I am a prince by birth and the gods are my brothers! Oh, so beautiful is the earth and so happy are the people!"

"How disgusting!" Adie repeated, hurriedly closing the website. "Does 'someone somewhere up there' think I would sell my soul for fame and money? So he makes me read that?"

She returned to the hallway, left her coat and hat, then went into the bedroom to change.

"Awful!" Adie continued to express her indignation to 'that so-and-so somewhere up there'. "You could have got me to read The Fart Olympics to make me laugh, instead of upsetting me with this insane story!"

The thought of The Fart Olympics brought a smile to her face. This poem had always succeeded in cheering her up no matter what the situation. . Since she had first read it years ago, she had recited it thousands of times to brighten her mood, to relax or just for fun. Adie had found it in an old newspaper. When she read it she laughed for hours, then she learned it by heart and she often recited it in front of the mirror artistically.

"Well, there's no need to read it. I know it by heart. Listen!" She turned again to the one above, standing half-dressed in her bedroom. Holding a sock in her hand, Adie began to recite it in her head, striking funny poses and gesturing animatedly.

Fart, my brothers, without constraint
And do not fret about complaints.
Do not worry about saving face
The job requires some open space.

Try different rhythms, try andante,
Then try piano, soft volante,
Frisky farting, allegro style,
Or a march that goes the extra mile.

To fart is art, a musical gift,

Make it a blast, do you get my drift?
Let rip your talent, no more concealing.
With charm and skill, express your feeling.

Be it solemn, be it festive,
A fart is more than just digestive.
It's a divine gift for deep expression.
Do not subject it to compression.

To silence a fart is a deadly crime,
To corrupt the rhythm or spoil the rhyme.
It censors what one freely thinks
And THAT's the thing that really stinks.

The fart is simple physiology.
What need is there for an apology?
A grand gesture, the fart is gallant,
With honour, chivalry ... even talent!

And ladies, be not faint of heart,
With joyful glee you must take part.
Not just at home, when out of sight,
Fart everywhere, both day and night.

Let's fart, my friends, in rhythm and rhyme.
Let's fart, fart, fart to the end of time.
And through our collective impropriety
Our farts will found a New Society

She was just bowing to her imaginary audience when her partner opened the door and asked:

"Are you going to be long?"

"I'm coming," Adie answered. She noticed his inquiring eyes. "Some coins fell out of my pocket and now I'm looking for them," she said in an attempt to justify her posture.

'This is the Smirnenski I like, why should you force those horrible things on me?" Adie again addressed the "man at the top", when her beloved had left the room. 'Well, it may be Penio Penev[6] who wrote it, but so what! It's a question of principle,' Adie raised her mental voice, as if "the superior one" corrected her for confusing the poem's author and she had to defend herself.

"Oh, come on! It's no big deal that there are no stairs in the poem. I'm sure that if there had been six-storey apartment blocks without elevators at the time Penyo Penev lived, he wouldn't have missed the opportunity to test the acoustics of the staircase. It's impossible not to fart at least once, especially when climbing them for the third time in a day, loaded down with heavy bags like a donkey," she continued her imaginary argument. "Now please, get away! I'm crazy enough without you to worry about too!" With that Adie terminated her dialogue with whoever was "above'.

"I am absolutely nuts", she thought while entering the dining-room to join her man. He was holding his drink with one hand and tapping nervously on the table with the other.

"Cheers!" He said, before she had even sat down.

"Cheers!" Adie raised her glass, sent him a kiss and took a sip of her favourite Mavrud[7] wine .

"What had to be checked so urgently?" he asked.

"A title of a book … otherwise I would have forgotten it," Adie improvised. She knew it would end in an argument if she tried to tell him about the veil exercise and all that had followed. Her attempts to share with him even the simplest episode from a seminar always led to a quite complex debate. Science and medicine were involved. Via psychiatrists, psychologists and of course Freud, it always ended the same way, with neither of them knowing precisely what they were arguing about. But they would fall out for at least half an hour.

There was tennis on the sports channel and, being his favourite sport Adie's beloved was immersed in the game, his questioning forgotten. As for Adie, she was staring at the TV without actually seeing it. Her mind was engaged with other things.

---

[6] Penio Penev (1930 – 1959) was a Bulgarian proletarian poet who glorified the building of socialism but later was disappointed with the new society and committed suicide.

[7] Mavrud is unique Bulgarian grape variety.

And if you find some stairs, brother,
Seek not for places other.
Take your chance and swiftly climb,
The acoustics are sublime!

"Ooh, I am good!" Adie commended herself with a complacent smile. "Hey, you there! That verse can go between the fourth and the fifth." She looked up again to the one above, but any reply of his was swallowed by a wide yawn that swept her face like a tidal wave. The meal and a glass of wine had made her feel drowsy.

"Phew, I feel exhausted today. I'm off to bed," Adie said aloud. She quickly got ready for bed, and the moment her head reached her pillow, she fell asleep.

6. CHAPTER SIX

The clanking of an early morning tram woke Adie. She thrust her hand beneath her pillow and fished out her mobile phone: there were ten minutes to go before the alarm.

Adie sensed some particularly nasty feeling inside her, and started wondering where it had come from. It wasn't the trams. The anger they used to provoke in her felt different. This feeling was more like torture, like guilt for something she had done wrong.

'The tale!' Adie suddenly remembered. This tale seemed to have affected her more deeply that she cared to admit. 'Is it really warning me about something?' she asked herself. 'Maybe at some point I really will find my vocation but may also drown in fame and money and become a vile snob?', she was thinking. 'I won't be able to see anything from the stairs … just as that young man was blind on the stairs… I may lose my sight and my hearing, my heart and soul', Adie continued talking to herself despairingly.

'Hey, thank you for warning me!' Adie abruptly addressed 'the thing" above that yesterday she'd held such an absurd dialogue with. Actually, she wasn't quite sure whether this "thing" was outside or inside her. Anyway, she added, almost tenderly: 'I promise I'll be very careful, really …'

Adie felt relief – as if she had managed to protect herself from some grave danger. At this moment the alarm on the mobile phone she was still holding started ringing. Adie quickly switched it off and slipped out of bed.

She went through her usual morning routine and set off to work. Today wasn't so bad - it was Friday. Adie loved 'the Friday feeling' It wasn't that two days off work were so near; having to go to work didn't bother her much. In any case, Adie was busy seeking her vocation in numerous other ways that she carried on working at the weekends. It was more the knowledge that there wouldn't be a wake-up alarm the next morning. Plus, on Friday evenings her favourite drama was on TV, another reason to smile and feel more relaxed on Fridays.

At work, Adie and her colleagues had what they called 'a Friday tease'. They had adopted a philosophy that Friday was a day to enjoy what they did. If someone was caught working too hard, they would soon be singled out: "Hey, easy there, it's Friday!"

When Adie sat at her desk and turned on her computer, she decided to check her email. Apart from spam, there were three messages from good friends. One of them lived in another town, the other was married to a foreigner and the third one was a foreigner.

"This is definitely a good day for me," Adie thought happily while wondering which email she should open first.

She picked the one from her friend who was in the country. They had never actually met and only knew each other by chance. This woman was a writer, and had sent Adie an article about the old tradition of fire dancing[8], thinking that she was sending it to some magazine. Adie read it. The writing was good. In fact Adie was so deeply impressed, she immediately replied to express her admiration for the author's talent. Many emails between them had followed, quickly revealing remarkably similar views and interests.

Adie particularly enjoyed emails from this friend. She always had something interesting to say. Today, however, her message was short, even though she had not written for some time. It turned out that her child was ill ... to make matters worse, she herself had fallen ill ... and now her husband was stuck in bed at home, having injections for bilateral pneumonia ... they were worried they might have made it worse by deciding to refuse to hospitalise him.

Adie swore. Then suddenly she screwed up her eyes, as she always did when she was struck by an interesting idea. Adie opened a new Word file

[8] Nestinarstvo is an old Bulgarian fire ritual that nvolves abarefoot dance on smouldering embers. The ritual is a unique mixture of Eastern Orthodox beliefs and older pagan traditions from the Strandzha Mountains.

and started writing.

For the kind attention of Mr ....
President of Healthy Body Ltd

Letter of Resignation

Dear Mr. President,
Please accept my resignation from my current position as illness at Healthy Body Ltd. I realise I have caused damage to the company and my resignation is the only act of honour I can think of.

I would like my resignation to be effective immediately and I promise I shall never approach this company again.

I wish only the best for you, and for the company.

Pneumonia Lungs-Bilateral

Adie emailed this to her friend, with instructions to fill in her husband's name at the top, as the president of Healthy Body Ltd. She must then print the letter, and get her husband to accept the notice by writing on it by hand, "Yes, I accept this resignation. To be dismissed immediately!" Then he must add the date, the time and his signature.

Next, Adie opened the email from her married friend. She was pregnant and complained of constantly being down in the dumps. Sunshine was the only thing that seemed to lift her, but it was a rarity in that country, especially at this time of year.

Adie rubbed her forehead. "Dear, dear! What can I do to help you?" The answer came in a second.

Adie remembered her friend's artistic talent; she loved to paint and make collages. She told her to find a picture of a sunrise and make it look like it was seen through a window by putting a frame round it. She could attach fabric, or even just a paper handkerchief, to make curtains.

Adie instructed her friend to open the curtain on awakening each morning. When she sees the sunrise, she had to say aloud: "What a beautiful sunny day it is!"

The third email, from her foreign friend, also began with a complaint.

This time it was due to a bad insomnia.

"For God's sake! What's going on?" Adie had been all set to enjoy the latest news from her friends, but they were all writing about their problems. Adie opened a new file and began to write again.

My dear,

Please forgive me for writing instead of telling you this personally, but I believe this way it will be easier for both of us.

I feel you are growing more distant from me, and I've noticed the obvious attraction between you and him...you know... Sweet Dreams. I don't want to get in the way of your happiness and comfort.

I wish you both a deep, lasting relationship. I hope he will give you everything your mind, soul and body may need. I am sure he will take good care of you and you will wake up every morning with a smile on your face; something I failed to give you.

You deserve to live every single day full of energy and joy. I am certainly not the one who can make you feel that way.

Please do not try to contact me.

Good bye!
Bad Insomnia

Adie saved that as Letter One, then opened another new document.

My dearest,

I hear from Aida that, after all these years with Bad Insomnia, he has left you.

The only way I see this is as a chance for you and I to do what we have been longing to do for so many years: to be together. I find it hard to hide my happiness that there will be no more lonely sleepless nights for you.

I can't wait to see you tonight, to hold you, to kiss your eyes, to tell you a wonderful good-night story, to watch over you while you are sleeping, to hear your calm breathing...

My dear, if you allow me, I'll come tonight. I'll wait in the dark in front of your house for a sign from you to come in and be yours. Please, if you want me tonight, before you go to bed go to your window. If I see you wave your hand, I will be there for you.

Yours forever,
Sweet Dreams

Adie saved this as Letter Two and attached it with Letter One to an email instructing her friend that she must open and read Letter One first, and only then read Letter Two.

'Bravo! I am very good today,' thought Adie with satisfaction, 'I didn't even need to think. Everything came so spontaneously to me,' she continued praising herself. 'Anyone else need a trouble shooter?' she mentally invited everybody who might have a problem to send it to her. Then she checked her inbox but it was empty.

"Well then, let's get some work done now." As Adie tried to focus on her computer screen, she remembered it was Friday, the day for indulging in one's favourite things. She decided to devote it to research on the company's soon-to-be-launched new product.

She began going through the scientific libraries of the World Wide Web's scientific libraries, looking for studies that could give her valuable ammunition for the marketing materials she would need to prepare later. She continued digging and reading, selecting information that she considered useful. After a few hours she decided she had done all she could and returned to her personal email: three new letters, from the same three friends as before waited in her inbox.

Her first friend had replied that, for the first time since they'd fallen ill, things seemed a little brighter, if only because Adie's letter had made them laugh so much. Her husband had already followed Adie's instructions, and they would keep her informed of any developments, Adie's friend promised.

The second friend had loved the task Adie had set her, and was enthusiastic to start. She promised to find some postcards with a sunrise, so she could make her window today.

The third friend wrote that she could hardly wait for the evening, to go the window and wave for *Sweet Dreams*. She assured Adie that she would write to her in the morning to tell Adie how *they* had spent the night!

Adie smiled. She was happy she was able to cheer her friends up and offer them something that they obviously liked to try. The rest depended on them. She thought again of how easily those ideas had come to her and began to wonder why it was that some days it worked out like that, while other days she felt blocked, unable to offer anything interesting.

Adie remembered something Alexey once said. Whenever he found himself in a position from which he could be of no use to his clients, he would just call them, cancel the session, and reschedule it for another day. Alexey had stressed that it was vital to extract oneself from the small socium position. Only then could one drop into the expanded position, the position one needed to be in to go with the flow and release the potential.

Adie realised that this morning she'd acted from the expanded position. She had not pushed herself at all, but something natural and spontaneous had occurred, channeled through her. She strongly suspected that this was something to do with the exercise with the veils from the previous night. Alexey had explained how its effects could be felt for some time, like an echo, in many different and unpredictable directions, until the echo faded away.

The ringing phone interrupted Adie's thoughts. It was a colleague from her former job who had also moved to the capital with his family. Adie loved being able to talk to him on the phone as well as see him often. He asked what plans Adie and her partner had for the weekend; the weather forecast was good and they intended to take advantage of what might be the last nice days before winter.

She had work planned for this weekend, but the idea of escaping the city was just too tempting. Adie adored the natural world. Whenever they got out in the open air she always went wild at first shocking the crowd.

If there was water nearby, Adie would be splashing in it. She would scoop up great handfuls and shriek as she threw the water high into the air, then laugh as the water rained back down all over her.

If there was a lawn, Adie would be crawling all over it. She'd sniff like a dog and roll over. "I adore the smell of grass and thyme," she would try to explain as others would guffaw, watching her blissful antics.

She also loved to run among the trees, randomly stopping at one to hug it, resting her head lovingly against its trunk. She'd stay like that, eyes closed, for a long time.

Sometimes she would just lie on the grass and contemplate the slow drift of clouds over the tree tops.

Adie quickly decided she could allow herself a weekend off. Her partner also endorsed the idea, and even gave a suggestion of where to go. Half an hour later it was sorted: early next morning they would be heading for a village in the mountains, fifty miles or so away from the city.

"Today really is a good day!" Adie affirmed to herself.

The working day was nearly over and, as it was Friday, Adie decided she could leave a few minutes early.

It was too soon though to go home. She had enough time to go to her favourite bookshop. Buying a "book for the soul", the kind of book that helped Adie give meaning of her existence, would be an appropriate ending to this lovely day.

She was already halfway there. When her bus stop came up, a crowd of people spilling from two other buses greeted her. . Adie mingled with the jostling pedestrians on her way to the traffic lights at the nearby crossing. Waiting for the lights to turn green, she heard a child's voice behind her, telling her grandfather:

"Grandpa, my teacher asked me what I wanted to be when I glow up …"

Adie turned quickly, absolutely sure that she would see someone pointing a finger at her, laughing. An old man and a little girl stood behind. The 'grandpa' looked at her blankly and focused his attention back to the girl.

'And what did you answer, sweetie?'

The peeps indicated that the lights had turned green. Adie turned and rushed across the street before she could hear the girl's answer. She then stopped at the other side to wait for the green lights at the next crossing, which lead to the bookshop.

'I thought we had sorted all this out! Please, stop walking behind and do not talk to me on the street, because I really will go mad…' Adie was almost pleading to 'the one above'. She thought that the morning's conversation had been their last.

"And, if you care to know, I've never got my 'l's and 'r's mixed up". Adie was

trying to prove that what she had just heard wasn't addressed to her. A group of teenagers on her left burst out laughing loudly. "Right, it is really funny that I've got such a wild imagination,' Adie told herself and a half-smile appeared on her face.

"Grandpa…, grandpa, I told the teacher that I still don't know what I want to be when I glow up…"

It was the little girl's voice. She hadn't been able to answer her granddad while they were crossing the street; now, 'by accident', they were there again, behind Adie.

Adie shook her head in disbelief and looked back. For a second, before the sound of the traffic lights and the hurrying people could sweep her away, her eyes met the little one's innocent gaze.

"At least you could have given me a sensible answer… not that silly 'I don't know", Adie accused 'the one above'. *'I don't know' can't be an answer… You 'don't know' when you're confused,'* she admonished that 'know-it-all".

At the moment it was easier for her to blame some outer force for sending her strange messages. She wasn't ready to accept that everything might have been happening inside her head and that she was somehow activating it.

She thought her last words should have snubbed the "superior". She quickly paced down the street, thus depriving "him" of any chance to answer.

She reached her favourite bookshop. The bell on the door welcomed her cheerfully. Adie loved coming here because she could look through the books without being disturbed. She could stay as long as she wanted, reading, without feeling obliged to decide quickly what she liked and buy. She went to her favourite section which was called 'Know yourself' and started looking through the rows of books, leaning her head to one side to read the titles.

Her attention was attracted by one of them – Awake for your Life's Purpose. She took the book out of the shelf, sat on the nearby chair, opened it at a random page and started reading:

Nowadays more and more people are wondering where exactly they 'fit' in the system, what the meaning of their life is and who they really are. If you also feel in this way, then, it's time to ask the most important question in life: Do you know who you really are?

"No," Adie said in passing and continued reading.

If the answer is 'NO' – congratulations!

Adie took her eyes off the lines with obvious bewilderment. After a moment, she turned her attention back to page:

Congratulations to you, not because of the courage to admit that you don't know who you are, but because the situation you find yourself in can help you as a starting point for discovering yourself. You might be surprised and you would may object that your confusion could not be a precondition for finding out who you are. But before you close this book disappointed, I would like to ask you to stay for a moment and think about this: what does it mean to be confused? 'I don't know who I am' is not confusion. Confusion is: 'I need to know who I am, but I don't'.

'Bless my soul!' Adie exclaimed to herself. She was petrified. For a moment she made an attempt to find some logical connection between all the strange things from the last two days – the staircase experience, the child, this book. The next moment she realized that if she continued looking for a rational explanation, she would burst into hysterical laughter. 'I'll call Alexey in a while,' she decided. She knew that he would offer some explanation – not "a logical one" of course, but from him, the 'crazy' interpretations sounded reassuringly normal. Now Adie was in a hurry to return to the text which intrigued her so much.

If you give up the belief that you must or need to know who you are, if you stop looking for definitions to give you a sense of your identity, what happens to your confusion? It suddenly disappears! When you fully and truly accept that you don't know who you are, you actually go into nothing. This "nothingness" brings you closer to realizing who you essentially are.

Adie fixed a dark stare on the wall in front of her. At yesterday's seminar Alexey had explained exactly this, but she obviously hadn't understood. The zero between the states was the permission they should give themselves not to know the solution of a given problem at a certain moment, so that they could find it after that. Adie thought that 'the nothing' she saw (or rather felt) from the stairs in her vision, was most probably her subconscious acknowledgement 'I don't know who I am'.

'I don't know what I want to be when I glow up' – the voice of the girl from the traffic lights resounded in Adie's head. 'He above' was right to mock

her. She was so convinced that when you 'had glown up', you should have defined yourself... and should know who you are, whether it be your true nature or not.

It seemed, however, that if someone wanted to find their real self, they should first lose what they believed it to be. 'I don't know' was not confusion but a state equivalent to 'zero'. From this state one could build whatever other state one wanted, as long as all constraints loaded by the socium and the need to determine oneself were removed.

'I can't believe what I've found!' Adie was in rapture over the book. Understanding that lack of knowledge didn't place her further away from her vocation but - on the contrary - brought her closer, filled her with great excitement.

Adie quickly stood up. Her finger lodged between the pages so she didn't lose what she had just read, she went to the cash-desk to pay for the book. She placed the receipt where her finger was, put the book in her bag and left the bookshop. Outside she stopped for a moment, lifted her smiling face towards the sky and shouted in her mind: 'Hey, you should know that you're terrible!' After a moment, realizing that she might be misunderstood by the "top guy", she added: 'I would like to say that you are awesome and I would like to thank you for helping me. You are very welcome if you visit me again' Adie was almost certain that she heard 'his' laughter. Or maybe it was her own, coming from her soul.

Adie dialed Alexey's number. His voice sounded agitated when he answered. He told her that he had just come out of a hospital, after visiting a client; a young boy whose mother had decided to take to a psychiatrist some time ago, despite Alexey warning her not to do so. The boy had been prescribed antidepressants and now he had fallen into a stupor[9].

"And what did you do?" Adie was intrigued how it was possible to help someone get out of this state, without using shock treatment.

"I just built a rapport[10] with him. For fifty minutes I mimicked his movements and followed his breathing. And when he moved his hand

---

[9] A condition of greatly dulled or completely suspended sense or sensibility.

[10] To build rapport means to enter someone else's world, to make him feel that you understand him, that you have a strong common bond.

slightly, I did the same. Then slowly, bit by bit, I brought him out of the stupor.

"Wow… doesn't sound easy!" Adie exclaimed.

"And see how your own mother can get you into trouble! Just because she takes it all too seriously. Anybody could fall into a stupor," Alexey was still emotional.

"Was the problem so serious that it needed a psychiatrist?" Adie couldn't work out what exactly had happened.

"Nothing dramatic. I spoke to the boy – normal teenage experiences but, as he was not open with her, she started worrying …" Alexey explained.

"Well… if she was worrying why didn't she go to a psychiatrist instead of taking the boy there? Adie asked.

"Because she didn't want to face her own fears. And as most people do, she found someone else to blame … The socium taught us to run away from ourselves and to look for excuses for our own experiences outside ourselves," Alexey answered and asked:

"Did you want to tell me something?"

"Yeaah" Adie drawled. She wasn't sure where to start, but decided to start from the beginning: "After the exercise with the veil all sorts of strange things started happening to me – it's very interesting, but a little crazy".

"For example?" Alexey encouraged her to continue.

Adie told him about "The Tale of the Stairs", today's story with the girl at the traffic lights and about the book in the bookshop, and finished:

"You remember I saw nothing from the stairs during the exercise? And that feeling of "nothingness" was weird. But it wasn't bad, I decided, just because there was nothing. Perhaps this was something which could help me: not knowing who I am and what I want to do might be the state I should start from in order to find my vocation.

"I don't know, Adie. We'll just have to wait and see." said Alexey.

"There's no way to explain what is what, because there is no such logic here. One thing is certain, however… you have triggered the potential and certain things have emerged."

"Quite shockingly in a way…" Adie added.

"Actually it's a lot of fun, if you forget the common view on normality and start trusting the flow of potential. It cannot hurt you, because at the level at which it manifests, 'evil' doesn't exist - said Alexey. "Call me to keep me up to date with what's going on," Alexey asked, before they ended the conversation.

Adie was still in front of the bookshop. On her way home she wandered around a couple of shops. When she saw delicious looking ready-meals in a take-away window display, she decided it was too late to cook for dinner and bought dishes for two.

Entering her block of flats, she saw a lot of bills and advertising flyers strewn on the floor. Adie sighed, knelt down and started sorting them into two piles, looking for those with their apartment's address on it. The moment she removed the last ones, she saw at the bottom, covered by the flyers and the bills, an A4 envelope, wrapped in transparent plastic. Below it, in large letters on two lines across the width of the envelope, was the following headline:

FIND THE MEANING OF YOUR LIFE

Adie was petrified, staring at this inscription in disbelief. She felt her right hand starting to ache; so hard was she clutching the letters and bills, as well as a flyer for some new supermarket. Holding her purchases in her left hand, she dropped the bills and the flyer on the floor and reached for the transparent envelope. It was hard to make out the addresses from such a distance. Her stomach tight, her mind blocked, her only thought was whether the recipient's name was her own.

Adie brought the envelope close to her eyes and saw that it was addressed to the youth organization whose office was on the third floor. She continued staring at the address, unsure if she felt relief or disappointment. On one hand, she wished it was her name there because this would prove that everything was directed by some outside force, sending her personal messages and clues to untangle and follow. Not that this would be easy, but she could always justify her belief by saying that the sign wasn't clear enough.

But the name on the envelope wasn't hers. Now she had to decide if the headline was a personal message to her or if it was just a letter. The things that were happening were shocking and normal at the same time. And Adie couldn't comprehend if they hadn't always been like this – containing in them both the natural and the supernatural and depending on the person himself to choose what to see in them.

A thought came into her head out of the blue; it was Einstein's and Alexey had quoted it to them at the first seminar: "There are two ways to live your life. One is to believe that there are no miracles. The other is to think that everything is a miracle."

Adie realised she had somehow landed on the first floor and was standing at the open window of the stairs overlooking a quiet inner yard.

'I didn't mean you should visit so soon,' Adie turned to 'the one above', this time consciously, while trudging up to the top floor. 'But I must admit it is more interesting with you,' Adie added.

She stopped on the third floor and attached the envelope to the door of the youth organisation.

When she got home, she first changed and then heated the meal she'd bought. Soon Adie and her man sat down to dinner, enjoying the usual Friday relaxed atmosphere and her favourite series. A new female character appeared and the leading man, for whom it was time to tie the knot, began chatting her up. The scene was in a bar and the man was asking 'probing' questions.

"What kind of work are you in?" he asked the woman.

"I haven't chosen any specific kind yet," she answered.

Adie bit her lips, to stop herself from laughing. "Hey! I'll get you for this!" she jokingly scolded her top friend. When the film ended she went to bed and tried reading but, feeling very tired, she snuggled up to her man and dropped off to sleep almost at once.

7. CHAPTER SEVEN

She woke up quite early for a Saturday, eager to leave for the mountains. At ten, the entire group departed, stopping a while at some point along the road. They arrived in the village at noon, dumped their bags at the hotel and walked to the village pub for lunch in its pleasant garden.

The sun was rather hot, an indicator that it might rain. Indeed, the forecast had warned of rainfall at high altitudes. Soon it became cloudy and the sun disappeared, but it was still pleasantly warm.

"Hope the rain holds off," Adie's friend said. They'd planned to walk after lunch.

"Don't worry!" Adie assured him, finishing a large glass of beer and feeling wonderful, physically and mentally relaxed, empty of thoughts and emotions. "I think this beer puts me directly into a superposition," she whispered softly to herself.

As soon as everyone was ready, they paid the bill and took off across the square, to a lane that led along the riverbank to a small waterfall. It was a typically fast-running mountain river, with many large stones that allowed it to be easily and safely traversed.

Adie could not resist the invitation of the stones for her to nimbly jump from one to the other. She squatted on one bigger stone which hampered the waterflow enough to form a small pool. She scooped up the water and threw it up, screaming with laughter like a child as it fell back over her. Her friends were laughing too, but at a safely dry distance from her.

When she'd had enough of this game, Adie rejoined her friends, thoroughly wet. She walked along with them a little, then dashed ahead when she saw the waterfall. Adie contemplated it alone for some time, filled with awe. The others arrived shortly and brought her out of her trance. They lingered there a little while, taking photos.

As they started to retrace their steps back to the lane, large rain drops began to fall. "It seems it will rain after all," stated the friend.

"It will only rain if we decide that we want it to rain," Adie said.

"Want it or not, it's started raining," said her partner.

The large drops became more frequent, bombarding them heavily whenever they emerged from under the trees.

"Lets run back to the pub!" said someone.

"Steady on. The rain's stopped," Adie said calmly. It did ease a touch. "The rain has stopped!" This time, Adie's voice was strong and commanding. At the same moment, the rain stopped, save for the occasional droplet.

"I told you it wouldn't rain," Adie said and turned to the group. "Is it OK now?"

"Perfect," the friend answered.

"If not, I can set it slightly harder," suggested Adie.

"Please, don't touch it any more!" the friend replied, laughing.

Adie was also grinning. The others, of course, thought it was just a coincidence that the rain stopped. None of them even considered the option that Adie might have had something to do with it. They simply accepted her words as one of her jokes.

"How perfectly this beer put me into the zero state!" thought Adie again. "I must tell Alexey." Then she realised, "But he surely knows. That is why he drinks beer all the time." Adie smiled. "I'll tell him that I have discovered his secret. He comes to the seminars already zeroed and covers us with handkerchiefs for fun, instead of giving us a beer too!" Her smile widened.

Adie had no doubt that she had stopped the rain. And this was not happening for the first time, but in other experiments it had taken her some time to enter the proper state. This time, maybe because of the beer she was in it already and did the "magic" very quickly.

They continued to walk slowly the whole afternoon, talking, and often stopping on the narrow path they were following. It led to a small chapel on the edge of a precipice. The sun was shining again adding soft nuances to the blended colours of autumn. It was beautiful, breathtakingly beautiful.

Adie had not brought her MP3 player, but in her mind she could hear very clearly Louis Armstrong singing *What A Wonderful World*, her favourite song for when she was moved by the beauty around her.

At the chapel, Adie stood for some time, contemplating the magical vista revealed to her eyes from this high place. Then she went to lie down on the grass in front of the chapel.

She thought about those righteous men who had once pinned their hope and their belief, and maybe their love on this chapel – on the edge of a chasm... 'They are always there – faith, hope and love – on the edge... It's so easy to fly off downwards and to be dashed into the abyss,' Adie thought, while her eyes tried to follow the faint movement of the clouds above her.

She had thought a lot about people and their various faiths. It seemed ridiculous that any religion could claim to be the only one and that those who followed other paths were doomed to eternal darkness, paying with hellish torment for their ignorance.

However, since she'd started to perceive existence as a choice that could be made and revealed at any time, Adie assumed that this choice applied also to religious beliefs about life after death. She thought it was quite possible for someone to obtain heaven after death, if they believed in heaven. If they believed in hell, they could go there instead. Those who believed in the eternal hunting fields would go to the eternal hunting fields. And those who did not believe in anything, they could receive nothing...

"Maybe, on the edge between life and death, a person enters a super-position, and the choices made at that moment become the new reality for them. Which also means one may choose to stay alive. That could explain why there are so many cases of people returning to life from near-death...making recoveries considered miraculous because they can't be explained scientifically," reasoned Adie.

This shocking idea occurred to her after she had read Shrodinger's cat –
one of the most popular mental experiments which tried to prove the
irrelevance of the quantum theory of the superposition, but which didn't
actually prove anything, in Adie's opinion.

The experiment revolved around an imaginary cat being placed in a
sealed box. In the box is a mechanism containing a radioactive nucleus and
a container with a poisonous gas. The parameters of the experiment are set
in such a way that there is a 50% chance for the nucleus to fission in one
hour. If this happens, the mechanism is activated, the container with the
poisonous gas is opened and the cat dies.

According to quantum mechanics, the result depended on the observer.
Before his observation, the nucleus was in a superposition, simultaneously
containing both future options – a nucleus which had fissioned, and a
nucleus which hadn't fissioned; and respectively, a dead cat and a live cat.
With his choice and expectations of the experience, the observer actually
defined the final result, namely 'the nucleus has fallen apart, the cat is dead'
or 'the nucleus hasn't fallen apart, the cat is alive'.

Alexey had related similar experiments which revealed that personal
expectations do influence a situation's outcome. Adie was very impressed
by the example in which three scientists conducting the same experiment
under exactly the same physical conditions received three completely
different results. The only difference in the experiment was the scientists'
attitudes and their expectations of the outcome.

It seemed that the Universe always confirmed what people believed in
and that one is always right.

"Do you believe in Hell? OK then, you're right. There is a hell and you
could go right there." Put another way: "Do you believe that your life is full
of problems? Then here you are: problems especially for you!"

It was getting darker. Adie perceived the breath of the earth under her
body – it was warm and wet, fragrant with herbs. The song of the crickets
in the grass around her caught her attention. She adored listening to them.
This was something she missed very much from her native town – the song
of the crickets in the summer coming through the open window. Adie
imagined that every evening they were gathering around her home to make
a serenade to her and she was eager to go to bed because of them.

Sometimes she woke up at night as if to make sure they were still there and she dropped off to sleep again when she heard they were.

'Nobody can glorify the grandeur and beauty of creation in a more virtuous way than these little musicians; not even Louis Armstrong.' Adie was enraptured, listening to the concert which was getting louder with the dark. 'This is for me the live Universe Alexey was talking about... I can feel the connection of everything... Every thing is both itself and everything else... And everything has meaning in an unconditionally clear way... And also it has its natural purpose.'

Adie's thought became somewhat weightless as if it wasn't coming from her but from somewhere outside. 'And why can't people be in that live Universe all the time? Why don't they want to be part of it but create some other external reality? Why do they refuse to be living beings but prefer to spend their lives as bio-machines in a mechanic Universe?' She was asking the questions with the strange feeling that it wasn't actually her querying. Somebody else inhabiting the space outside her was noting that people are wasting their existence.

Her mind relaxed more and more. She felt as if she was sinking down into the soft grass and dissolving in the sounds of the crickets, in the scent of herbs, in the cool air caressing her face, in the Earth's breath she felt through her clothes. She felt she was disappearing, but without losing herself. On the contrary, she was becoming everything, the whole world itself, completely and fully.

Her friends' laughter reached her mind, but somehow at a distance. She heard her name and opened her eyes reluctantly. Her beloved was leaning over her.

"Don't lie on the ground, Adie, you may catch a cold," he said with concern, holding out his hand to help her up.

She had no idea how much time had passed. She realized that she had had no sense of time in this state, which was different from the zeroing that she had experienced so far. In a way it was like the feeling at the exercise on volume perception of reality. They had often done this at seminars in order to "expand", Alexey's way to describe leaving all the time and space constraints of the linear universe.

Unwillingly Adie held out a hand to her man and stood up. Still in her reverie, she followed him to the bench in front of the chapel where their friends were. She felt cold and snuggled in his arms to warm up. After a while they set off back to the village. The fresh air and the walking had obviously tired them and they decided to have dinner in the restaurant of the hotel to be near their beds when they got sleepy. They were sitting relaxed on the chairs, sipping slowly from their drinks, enjoying the feeling that they didn't need to do anything or to hurry anywhere. They weren't even talking, just exchanging calm smiles. The light music suddenly stopped and all the customers lowered their voices on an impulse.

"I know…let's tell funny stories that have really happened to each of us," Adie suddenly interrupted the silence on their table, smiling widely.

The others laughed.

"How did you come up with that?" her loved one remarked.

"OK, but you start first," her friend set down a condition.

"No problem" Adie agreed, thoughtfully scratching her head.

Everybody was staring at her, expecting to hear some of her funny stories. Nobody was sure if they were absolutely real or she was making them up but she was well known for her imagination.

"Oh, yes!" she exclaimed after a while, almost jumping from the chair. "I'll tell you a "lost in translation" true story.

Her friends urged on her impatiently.

"When I was abroad…" Adie started, but then stopped to explain: "You know that several years ago the company sent me abroad with a big group of people. I was in charge of them as I was the only person who knew a little English at that time."

The others nodded and Adie continued:

"So, we got there, the people welcomed us and after we had settled down, they informed us about some things that we should know. One of them was that we should have a medical examination; that was standard. I asked them what these examinations were and they explained they would be very simple: checking weight and blood pressure and doing the 'water test'. I didn't understand what the 'water test' was but it sounded harmless. I didn't ask what it was because I didn't want them to think that we had grown up in the wild and had never had a 'water test'. But then my people started asking *me* what the test was like. As I didn't want *them* to think I didn't get it because of my poor English, I had to give some explanation."

Adie paused. So far her expression had been serious but now smiles began to flash on her face.

"And what did you tell them?" her friend urged her to continue.

"Well …I explained to them very seriously …" Now she altered her voice to sound serious and competent and recited: "You can see that in this country it constantly rains. It's a pity to see so many disabled people. Poor them, they can hardly walk, and many use wheelchairs…This is because of the rain and the high humidity. That's why here they have a special examination: a water test, which they do to everyone to check if they retain water."

The laughter burst out irresistibly.

"And that's not all," Adie said, as she was trying to drown out the laughter.

"I explained to my people in great detail how they would tap on us with small hammers to see if we had collected water somewhere in our bodies."

There was another burst of laughter.

"That's not a real story," her friend could hardly articulate while he was drying up the tears on his face.

"It's true my dear, it's true." Adie stressed. "And what's more: I must have been so convincing that everybody believed it. And I even believed it myself."

"What did this water test turn out to be at the end?" her friend's wife asked when the laughter had subsided.

"You'll find out when you hear the end of the story," Adie answered.

"Oh, there's more!" her friend was glad to hear there will be more.

"Yes, the funniest part," Adie answered, quite pleased she had made them laugh that much. "So, one day we went to the consultation room and everything started as expected. I, of course, being in charge, went through the check ups first. So they weighted me, took my blood pressure and then it was time for the water test. I expected a doctor with a hammer to appear, but instead a nurse brought me a plastic cup, muttered something from which I only got 'water test' and pointed to a door on the other side of the room.

I later understood it was a toilet door; next to it there was a wash-basin. Without really knowing why, I went to the wash-basin, ran the water and filled the cup. When I turned back to bring her the water, I saw the nurse looking at me open mouthed and after a moment she doubled up with laughter.

The company burst out laughing.

"Just when she said 'urine' it dawned on me that water test was simply a urine test."

"Well, didn't you realize when she gave you the cup?" her friend's wife asked.

"Not at all," Adie answered. "This was at the time when, here, we gave urine samples in small brown bottles with narrow throats. So we always peed on our hands."

The group burst out laughing again.

"That's true," the woman confirmed.

Adie suddenly became serious and said in a sad voice:

"Actually this story is as funny as it is sad. Later I realized that the reason you see so many disabled people in that country was not the rain but the fact that these people could get out of their homes and move around whenever they wanted. The state had made this possible for them and enabled them to live normal and fulfilled lives. Here there are no fewer people with disabilities but we just don't see them. The state has doomed them to imprisonment in their homes and it hasn't created even the most elementary conditions for them to be able to move out."

Everybody's faces darkened.

"Let's hope this changes soon – we are becoming Europeans aren't we?

Now, whose turn is it?" Adie urged her friends to take the baton. Her friend raised his hand and announced in a triumphant voice:

"I'd like to tell you how once I pinched a mafioso's bottom."

The company burst out laughing again.

"Come on! And you are still alive?" Adie's man exclaimed.

"I was on the verge of death," her friend said, laughing. "I have an enormous colleague with a shaved head. If you don't know him you will take him for the typical local crook, but he only looks like one, otherwise he is very kind and funny. Once he was telling a joke about homosexuals as he was doing impressions of typical gestures they do in a really high-pitched voice. As he is very big and macho it was really funny. Since then it has become a joke to slap and to pinch him on the bottom whenever we see him."

The group made approving noises.

The man continued, "So, one day entering the supermarket, I suddenly saw my colleague, just in front of me, in the queue. I went right up to him and started pinching him on his bum."

Everybody burst out laughing.

"And, what happened…?" someone impatiently urged him to continue amid everybody's giggles.

"And when the guy turned around, I saw a complete stranger, glaring at me. I had the feeling he was going to crush me on the spot. I virtually bent over backwards and I could only say: "Sorry, I must have mistaken you for somebody else", which sounded absolutely ridiculous.

The rest burst out laughing again.

"Yes, it is crazy to pinch somebody's bottom in a shop queue and then say that so sheepishly… it sounds like a scene from a cartoon," Adie commented after she was able to stop laughing for a while and reached to take a clean napkin for her running nose and eyes.

"And how did you manage to get out without being killed? Adie's boyfriend asked.

"I have no idea, even now… Maybe I looked extremely pitiful and that's why he spared me. I got off with just some interesting ideas about what would happen to my 'homo ass' if he got a grip of it." The friend answered which was met by another burst of laughter.

"Oh, I need more air," Adie said while she was breathing deeply to calm down.

They filled their glasses with wine from the jug and proposed a toast. Their eyes were sparkling, full with laughter.

"Whose turn now?" Adie asked, looking meaningfully at her man and at her friend's wife.

"Mine," the latter said.

This lady was normally quite restrained. After her family's move to the capital she had found a responsible managerial position in a big company and obviously she took this quite seriously. Adie sometimes wondered what connected the two of them as they were clearly quite different. But they probably complemented one another well because they got on well. Adie was curious to hear her version of 'a funny story'. When in company, the woman always laughed at the silly jokes the others shared but she herself never volunteered any.

"Well, once I went to a yoga class …" the woman started.

"Very funny!" her husband whispered to the others, joking at her seriousness. "But you gave it up after the first time," he said loudly, suddenly remembering the case.

"Yes, but now I'll tell you why," she answered with a mysterious smile and began the story: "I was full of enthusiasm, after I'd read all sorts of information about how healthy and useful it was for the body and spirit and so on. Obviously it was the thing to do in those days, as the group was big, maybe 40 people."

"That's a lot!" Adie exclaimed. "Where did they fit you all in?"

"In a large hall near our home, with very good acoustics," the woman answered.

"What did you need the acoustics for? To sing mantras or what?" her husband kidded.

"Stop interrupting me and you'll find out," she grumbled jokingly. She sipped from her wine and added: "If I wasn't drunk like this I would never tell you this terrible story."

"Oh, that's a bit of a teaser. Go on, darling…" her husband urged her.

"It's a bit embarrassing, I'd say." She took a deep breath, waved her hand as if to say "anyway" and told them her story.

She went to the yoga class, put her mat on the floor and diligently started doing the exercises, as shown by the instructor. One exercise involved stretching her legs up which is when she sensed air coming in, between her legs. When she brought her legs down, the air was forced out, with a sound as loud as a farting horse.

"With those acoustics, it was truly terrible," the woman finished her story. "Can you imagine what the other people thought? Probably: "Wow, she farts like a trooper!" she finished while her friends were almost in hysterics. Adie squatted down – she did this when she had the feeling that if she didn't bend over, her spleen would burst. After a while she climbed back up on the chair and confessed with sincere rapture:

"Oh… that is the best! You really kill me!"

"Well, didn't you do anything to explain yourself?" the woman's husband asked.

"What could I do? Stand up in front of the crowd and to cheerfully inform everybody: 'Ladies and gentlemen, that wasn't a fart. My vagina just sucked up some air'."

The laughter erupted with new force. When everybody calmed down, they turned to Adie's partner. He was the only one who hadn't told a story. At that moment, concentrating hard, he was trying to cut a piece of the cold steak in front of him, pretending not to notice their looks. But under the pressure of their glances his hand trembled, the knife slipped and the big piece flew high into the air in an arc, and landed right in the empty plate of a man sitting at the table next to theirs.

For a while both parties remained in awkward silence. Adie and her friends looked embarrassed at their 'neighbours', expecting some reaction.

It didn't take long. The people at the other table turned their heads simultaneously. For a second both companies stared at each other, then they all burst out laughing, which made the other customers turn their heads to see what was happening. The man who 'received' the stake 'from above' stood up, went to Adie's table and asked who was the master of that performance. Everybody pointed at her man because they couldn't speak from laughter. The man shook his hand and congratulated him on the superb shot.

"This was like a scene from Charley Chaplin's movie," remarked the friend when he was able to speak again.

"A genius act," his wife agreed.

Adie was still giggling. She bent towards her dearest and kissed him on the cheek.

"I beat you all, didn't I?" he said proudly, satisfied with his performance.

"My sides split from laughing," her friend's wife said.

"Yes… and my stomach," Adie could hardly speak, still smiling widely.

They stayed for a while, until the wine was finished among jokes and laughter and, when they saw that midnight had passed, they decided to go to sleep.

'I don't remember the last time I laughed so much from the bottom of my heart,' Adie thought while she was brushing her teeth in front of a big mirror in the bathroom. Suddenly she stopped rubbing her teeth, took the toothbrush out of her mouth and brought her face closer to the mirror. She smiled slightly and touched the fingers of her free left hand to the skin around the outer corner of her eyes – first the left eye, and then the right one.

She loved the idea of having wrinkles of laughter around her eyes when she was older, and she often checked whether they had already begun to form. Adie believed that a sense of humour and our ability to laugh was the strongest proof of human divine origin. 'They can try to explain everything as chemical, biological, physical and all sorts of logical scientific laws. Even love. But all arguments about the simian origin of man go out the window when he laughs," Adie ruminated. She believed that laughter has extraordinary purifying and reviving power and it was one of the things that immediately attracted her to Alexey's seminars.

While looking in the mirror Adie heard snoring sounds coming from the room. As she was with toothbrush in one hand and her mouth full of toothpaste, she nipped across through the bathroom and the hallway and stopped in front of the bed. Her dear was already sleeping and snoring soundly.

'Right, I forgot to tell the doctor that we were going away,' Adie reproached herself, padding back to the bathroom to rinse her teeth. She wondered what to do – she didn't want this "soundtrack" to spoil her whole experience. Settling in bed she remembered one of the first exercises they did at the seminar: to thank the problem that plagued them, but in a specific way. First she had to give it a name and Adie spontaneously called it 'Unufrie'. Then she mentally expressed her gratitude: "Thank you, Unufrie, for warning me that by snoring, you will ruin my sleep and I'll stay goggle-eyed and awake all night, listening to the crickets and planning how to crush their violins into your head."

Then she had to give 'a present' to the problem. "And by expressing my gratitude, I wish you a deep sleep in silence and I give it to you…" Adie stopped in the middle of the sentence and thought. The present was an important thing, as it had to be liked by the problem. "And I give it to you in the form of a firefly in a ball gown, playing Rachmaninoff[11] on a white grand piano." Adie finished and held her breath. Her man snored once louder, grunted and subsided.

"Wow, that was quick," Adie was stunned but very pleased with her achievement. But she didn't have energy left to reason. All the stories they had been telling each other that night had been passing through her mind in quick succession. She laughed silently several times and soon fell asleep with a blissful smile on her face.

---

[11] Sergei Vasilievich Rachmaninoff (1873 –1943) was a Russian composer, pianist, and conductor. Rachmaninoff is widely considered one of the finest pianists of his day and, as a composer, one of the last great representatives of Romanticism in Russian classical music.

8. CHAPTER EIGHT

The next morning they enjoyed another walk, but after a leisurely lunch it was time to head back for the city. Despite two relaxing days, Adie felt tired when they arrived home. Her remaining energy was sapped just by loading the washing machine and preparing a simple supper. As soon as the washing machine finished, she crawled off to bed to read.

The phone rang and her man answered it. From what he said, Adie realised that it was her painter friend calling. He was the most interesting respondent from all the people Adie had interviewed about the meaning of life. She had done so often recently: asking people she met, no matter whether they were old friends or recent acquaintances, if what they were doing was their vocation.

She was surprised to find out that most people didn't have her problem. She could understand those who said that what they were doing was what they had always wanted to do. But she couldn't understand the others who were surprised at her questions because they had never thought about the meaning of their lives.

However, she had never discussed her biggest question with someone like the artist. He said he never doubted what his vocation was. Painting was his entire life; it inspired, motivated and gave him a sense of purpose. He didn't need to choose what to do. Adie wasn't that surprised by the answer, but it confused her further.

It seemed as though his vocation was given to him at birth. He wasn't looking for it – he had simply followed it. She wondered whether this could be applied to all people. Maybe some of them - like her – had just let the moment to spot and follow it pass them by.

'And maybe I just have to look back and find that moment when I overlooked my vocation,' Adie thought.

Tonight, the artist had phoned to invite Adie to his one-man exhibition, which he had titled *The Second Calling*. The word 'calling' was enough to stir a tremble within Adie, but hearing it combined with 'second' was too much for her. "I don't know who this wag thinks he is," Adie complained to herself in her thoughts, "nor why he thinks he can make jokes at my expense: inviting me to an exhibition of his second calling when I have yet to find my first!" Adie felt peeved.

The artist had named his exhibition *The Second Calling* because he was presenting his own translations of poetry, along with his illustrations painted specially for them.

"I envy him," Adie's thoughts continued as she closed her eyes for sleep. "He must feel really happy, to be doing things that are to him his essence." Then a question caught Adie by surprise. "And what actually is essence?"

The question rankled Adie, despite the relaxed warmth of her bed. She felt sure she must have studied the concept of essence, but could not remember any definition. Right now, she needed one more than anything. She felt sure that this definition, if there was one, would help her shape the vague feeling of who she was at her core.

Adie simply had to find an answer. She abandoned her bed and climbed on a stool to retrieve her philosophical dictionary from the top bookshelf.

"What are you up to now? Why aren't you sleeping?" asked her partner.

"I have to check the meaning of a word," Adie explained.

"I see," he sighed, as if it was perfectly normal for her to consult the philosophical dictionary during the night. He was resigned to her oddities.

Adie returned to bed, opening the volume. Leafing through its pages, she stabbed her finger into "E", and dragged it down the page ...

ESSENCE The attribute or set of attributes (properties, qualities) that make an object or substance what it fundamentally is. That which it has by necessity, and without which it loses its identity.

"That's it!" exclaimed Adie in her mind. "I have lost the original identity that was me, fundamentally, utterly, fully… I have replaced it with other identities that are not me. That is why I have the feeling of being multiple, because I am not me!"

Adie dropped the dictionary onto the heap of books by her side of the bed, switched off her reading lamp and slid under the blanket.

No more that 10 seconds later she reached out, switched on the lamp again and took the new book she had bought on Friday. She opened the page marked with the receipt from the bookshop and read the first paragraph she came across.

When you don't know who you are, in practice it doesn't matter what you do – anyway, you are not yourself. What really matters is whether you identify yourself with what you do to a degree that it becomes a role that you play and you mistake the role for the essence. If what you do when you are not yourself turns into a role, it means you mistake a model of behaviour for who you are in reality and you take yourself seriously.

'Exactly!' Adie exclaimed to herself. She closed the book and put it next to her pillow instead of on the heap of books.

'That's what I do all the time – I rush to do things, identify myself with many different activities and turn them into roles … And all the time I consider the roles I play are me, while in fact they are taking me away from myself. And when I delude myself in this way everything becomes extreeemely serious, extraooordinary important and hooorribly tough!' Adie was talking to herself while she was settling under the blankets. She reached for the reading lamp above her head again and switched it off. But her mind was so awake that it didn't let her sleep.

'Well,' she continued pondering, 'how can I know when what I do is not a role but is the real thing, revealing my essence?' Once again she switched on the light, pulled herself up slightly, took the book and opened it at random. Her man cast a long glance at her, without saying anything. Adie didn't notice at all. She was reading:

When you are not playing role you are fully concentrated and absorbed in your work. You've become one with it. When a person is in that condition, he might not realize it but what he is doing turns into a spiritual activity, into worship.

'Amazing!' Adie was astonished. 'Well, it's right under my nose. So simply and clearly explained! What a magic book! It contains the answers to all my questions! OK, then! Let's check if it tells me what I'll be when I 'glow' up.' Adie smiled. She was satisfied with the answers she had received that evening and this was like teasing 'the guy up above", who she believed was giving them. She closed the book and then again opened it randomly – at another page. The following paragraph jumped out at her.

"Zen reads: 'Don't look for the truth. Just stop asking for opinions'. Adie laughed freely, which startled her dear one.

"Oh!" he exclaimed and reached under the covers to pinch her in revenge.

"Sorry, great jokes here." Adie decided that it was better to spare him how she played oracle with the book.

He turned back to the TV and continued watching. Adie turned back to the book and read the other two sentences in the paragraph:

Stop defining with your brain. Then who you are, beyond the mind, will reveal itself.

Adie closed the book slowly and dropped it on the others.

'*Stop defining with your brain...*' She repeated to herself, settling comfortably under the blankets. She switched off the bedside lamp again. '*It will reveal itself ...*'

A smile spread across her lips and a moment later, still smiling, she fell asleep.

9. CHAPTER NINE

Monday began with the wake-up alarm. Adie stretched as she slipped out of bed feeling fully refreshed and rested, in contrast to most mornings. "I must spend time with Nature more often. It energises me so much!" she thought.

Adie took her new feeling to work with her, but as she switched on her computer she realised her mood was not one for work; she was still cosily wrapped inside her feeling of relaxation from the weekend. She pondered which task would require least effort.

Her Skype messenger caught her eye with a new message alert. Opening the chat window revealed that it was from someone unknown. Adie felt uncertain. She used Skype mostly for work purposes, occasionally to exchange brief words with friends, but generally she disliked 'chat' and was usually careful to reset her status as 'not available'. She always ignored strangers who weren't in her contact list.

But Adie was intrigued by this message. It was a touch longer than the usual cues strangers sent. Reluctantly, Adie felt drawn to read it.

"If today were my last day," the stranger had written just a few minutes ago, "I would still message you. Good morning! It was a nice surprise to read your motto on your profile."

Adie tried to remember what she had put in her profile. It took her some time to even navigate to the right screen, but eventually she found what she had written as her motto:

"If you live every day as if it were your last,
one day most certainly you will be right.
If today was the last day of your life,
would you still want to do
what you are about to do?"

"I must have been nuts when I wrote this!" thought Adie, although she quite liked the idea, and it certainly applied today. She decided that her lack of enthusiasm for any serious work was sufficient excuse to follow her curiosity and spend some time chatting with this stranger.

"Good morning!" Adie typed, "I'm glad to be reminded to ask myself if today will be my last day." A few moments passed. She added, "But I deeply hope that it won't be!"

"Why?" the stranger asked.

"Because I am not ready to answer the challenge. I have to do a mountain of things that I don't want to deal with at all. Do you always do only what you want?" Adie returned the question.

"Not always. But today, yes. That's why I am talking to you right now, I want to and I like it," answered the stranger.

Adie was picking up speed. "Tell me, have you at least always been aware of what you really would want to do?"

"No. Sometimes it takes me a while to figure it out," was the answer.

"For me this is a serious problem. My mind and my heart often disagree." Adie was no longer able to hold back. Here was someone who wanted to talk to her … even if it was the last day of their life … and was interested in her favourite topic.

"It's not that serious with me, but I know what you mean. What is your biggest doubt right now?" the stranger asked.

"That's very complicated" Adie gave a vague answer and switched to another question. "Do you laugh often?"

"Quite often, at work and outside work. But it's not my habit. I've just been lucky to live a life that allows me to laugh often," the stranger replied, not seeming to mind Adie's evasion.

"I would like to laugh more often. I'm too serious!" Adie wrote, adding a sad face emotion. "Laughing is good... cleans the ego. Ego makes us unhappy."

"Same here. I'm no clown, but around me are people who help me laugh more often than I would without them."

"What makes you feel happy?" Adie asked.

"People! Always people, never property or money. I like people most and I feel happy with people."

"I think that nobody and nothing can make us happy if we lack the right inner attitude for happiness," Adie commented.

"Absolutely!"

"The outer world can add to our happiness to some degree, but can't make a happy person out of an unhappy one," Adie claimed.

"But I've never met anyone who is a totally unhappy person. I've only seen people who are just not feeling happy in their current situation." To Adie, his words sounded rather like an excuse.

"Lucky you! Until today. You have just met one really unhappy person." Adie realised her statement sounded quite melodramatic.

"Fine," he said, in a conciliatory tone. "I met you and it felt really nice. What am I to do now? Get infected by your unhappiness? Run away? Stay neutral? ... I choose to enjoy your company and our conversation." A smiley face was added. Adie delayed answering, so the stranger continued.

"We can talk about your unhappiness, if it's not too personal for you."

"Which planet have you fallen from?" Adie thought to herself as she wrote, "Are you sure you are not confusing happiness and satisfaction? Happiness is attitude that comes from finding MEANING."

"Maybe you feel like that because you are at a crossroads? You need to choose between total responsibility for everything you experience and feel, or make someone else responsible. I'd guess you generally don't trust anyone but yourself?" The stranger offered his conclusion in his question.

"I am aware that what I feel and experience is my responsibility, but sometimes, when we choose our own happiness we may hurt other people," Adie pointed out.

"Indeed, choosing our own happiness can affect other people, but it's also their choice whether they are happy or not, no matter what we have or haven't done."

Adie realised that maybe she was not finding her vocation because she was unconsciously resisting it, fearing that if she found it and followed it she might hurt others around her, or at least disappoint them in some way. She continued the exploration. "True, but we're so trapped in social and personal norms of behaviour that sometimes it's very difficult to see the choice, let alone make it."

"Should I take it that the environment in which you live puts pressure on you not to make the choice and the change that you would like to make?" the stranger probed.

"Maybe, a little bit. But things are never just black and white, and shades are often more important than the basic colours," Adie answered.

"But sometimes that pressure also is just what you perceive, and not always an actual pressure," the stranger pressed, then further, "Maybe you should work on your perceptions rather than trying to change the circumstances or trying to meet the demands of others?"

"Hah, you really are a smart cookie!" Adie thought, impressed by his point. While she was wondering what to say, another message came:

"If you're not sure, you can try the opposite. Just stop searching for a while. Simply satisfy the desires of others and let circumstances lead you. But do that sincerely and completely. Then you will better understand what you want and why you want it, after you first understand 'black' completely. Then, when you choose another colour, it should be easier: you would only need to choose the road that leads you from black to that colour."

Adie, reading quite carefully, was increasingly impressed by what the stranger wrote. "Are you a psychologist?" she asked.

"No, I am a decision maker," the stranger answered, "I teach and I consult."

"I study psychotherapy," Adie matched.

"Perhaps we could try a one-to-one session and test our skills on each other?" the stranger proposed. "I'll practice decision making on you, and you practice psychotherapy on me. It might prove to be quite interesting!"

"Sorry, but this sounds as if I'm talking to an internet pervert!" Adie added a smiley face to soften her joke.

To her surprise he answered: "You got me! That's what I am. You are a clever psychotherapist. I'm glad you found me out. I'm nothing but a pervert. But wouldn't you like a one-to-one session anyway?"

Adie felt shock. "No, perversion is not something we share in common." Adie was angry that their pleasant talk had suddenly turned into complete insanity. She hung on only because it had not yet sunk in that it was true.

"Nice way to decline a chance of a lifetime," conceded the pervert, adding in brackets, "(By the way, I would not be allowed to teach if I was a pervert.)"

"Only if they knew about you," countered Adie. "Perverts are usually good at concealing themselves." She added, "I don't know why I have not blocked you yet!"

"Pervert is a label assigned by others and is only a matter of perception. In theory, you may define me as a pervert and block me out at any moment. But that is irrelevant to whether I am a pervert or not. Your decision to block me would be a choice based only on your perception."

"My perception is based on my values and beliefs," Adie asserted.

"So? Your choice would be based on your values and beliefs." The stranger then added, "I shall have to leave in twenty minutes. I'm telling you that so we can finish this conversation in a non-abrupt way. Would you take a risk and ask me ten questions before we finish? Then decide if you want to add me to your contact list or not?"

"Okay, but I don't have time now. Can we talk again later?" Adie was still intrigued.

"Is this our last day?" the stranger asked for an answer.

"No, I don't believe so," Adie said.

"I do," the stranger informed her. "This may be the last day, and it would be my choice to spend it all with you entirely, if we both agree that it must be our last day."

"Why?" Adie wanted to know.

"Because you are a great conversationalist," the stranger offered.

"Could conversation be the meaning of life?" Adie provoked.

"No, it is not the meaning of life," the stranger conceded. "But it is very important, and on the last day it would be the most important thing." He went on, "You have implied that this won't be our last day. So I won't spend it with you. But I am an optimist and I will enjoy it nevertheless. It really was very nice to talk to you and I appreciate your optimism that there will be other opportunities to talk."

"I am adding you to my contacts list," announced Adie. "Thank you for the idea that you would spend your last day with me, I take that as a compliment!"

"I like your attitude!" the stranger confessed.

"Must cancel now. Talk soon. Take care." Adie was determined to end the conversation now, having suddenly noticed that over an hour had passed.

"You take care too," replied the stranger, and the conversation was off.

"That was certainly a fresh way to start a new week," thought Adie, feeling satisfied.

It wasn't until 81 days later that Adie realised the stranger had never reappeared online again. She noticed the name by chance while looking up another friend from her Skype contact list. She clicked on it and began to reread the dialogue they'd had, gradually realising that maybe that day was indeed the stranger's last.

Adie felt the discomfort that always seized her when the question of death was raised. Despite her effort not to think about it, her mind was invaded by questions about whether this person really was dead and what it was to realize that maybe in a month, day, hour, 20 minutes and 30 seconds, you wouldn't be in this world anymore.

At this very moment the thought of how she would spent her day, if it were the last one, no longer seemed so hypothetical. Perhaps because, realizing that this man might have died, she suddenly felt as if she truly had participated in a last day. "He was on the verge of death, and I behaved as if doing an abstract exercise from a book of popular psychology," Adie thought. Suddenly she was gripped by panic.

The thought of death obscured any sense of meaning; what's more, it seemed to stultify her searching for it. She called Alexey to tell him how futile she felt. Without even thinking, he suggested she change her perspective toward eternity: "Just, change the question, Adie – Alexey said. "Instead of asking what you would do if today was your last day, ask yourself what you would do if you were immortal." Adie would hug him if he was near. In the context of eternity her calling suddenly acquired even greater importance and turned into an exciting challenge.

After she finished her conversation with the stranger, Adie had the best of intentions to get down to her work. But then she remembered that she hadn't checked her e-mail since Friday and decided to do so first. All three of her girlfriends for whom she'd set tasks had replied over the weekend.

She eagerly opened the one from her friend whose husband was suffering from pneumonia. He had managed to get out of bed the next day after signing the resignation letter, and was even able to do some work. The doctor they visited that morning was amazed; she had never seen such a rapid and complete recovery from pneumonia.

Adie's friend concluded her email by saying she was just writing to let Adie know about the situation, but that she could not comment on any connection between her husband's recovery and Adie's 'prescription'. Adie didn't know what to make of it either; she hadn't expected any particular result from Pneumonia's letter of resignation. She simply replied that she was happy to hear of the speedy recovery.

Next, Adie opened the email from her foreign friend. Insomnia was no longer troubling her. She still woke up a few times during the night but easily managed to fall asleep again, which was definitely a new experience for her. She added that she liked to imagine that she was lying in the arms of her new love, Sweet Dreams.

This prompted Adie to suggest a new bedtime ritual to her friend. The symbolic gesture of waving her hand at the window was no longer necessary. Instead, Adie suggested she should imagine that Sweet Dreams had permanently moved in with her. Another symbolic act, such as combing her hair before going to bed, would show him that she needed him and was preparing herself especially for him.

In the third email, Adie's pregnant friend was thrilled by the task Adie had set her. It put her in a great mood each time she raised the curtain … several times a day … to see the sunshine outside. Adie told her to raise the curtain once each morning, and fix it so that the sunshine could enter all day long, and to drop the curtain only at night.

Despite having had the very best intention to tackle her work, lunchtime arrived as Adie sent the last email to her friend. She went out to get something to eat, firmly resolving that after feeding herself she would settle down to some serious work. But the arrival of a new email thwarted her. It was an invitation to take a test to evaluate her best career options. Some time ago Adie had registered on a website offering this free service, and she'd lost count of how many times she'd been offered the chance to test different aspects of her personality.

There had been a time when Adie had loved taking such tests. She had been keen to get to know herself better and see herself objectively so that she could improve her personality. But she was soon disillusioned. The questions were always too general. Adie wanted, if her own individuality was going to be assessed, to have a specific evaluation of her identity as a unique human being. Besides, she had found that if she took the same test on two different days, when she was in a different mood, the results varied widely despite it being the same Adie the test referred to.

The last test she had taken was to measure her IQ. That was a funny story. Later she was tempted to repeat the test to verify the accuracy of the results, but decided to hold on to the illusion of her own super-intelligence. She had scored 157 points.

At first, Adie was clueless about what the points meant. For some reason, she had believed that to demonstrate an average intelligence she had to score at least 300 points. On that basis, 157 points came as a shameful demoralisation to Adie, smashing to pieces her long-held belief about how smart she was.

Adie stumbled around clearly crestfallen, but it was several days before a friend took her for a coffee and discreetly enquired if there was a problem. Hesitantly, Adie decided that she might trust him with a confession of her shameful secret.

"Well," she began, "I've discovered that I am not as clever as I thought I was."

"And what's made you think that?" asked her friend.

"I took an IQ test." Adie dropped her gaze for a moment, before she looked up with tears ready to stream down her face. "My score was... 157 points." Blushing heavily, she looked down at the floor.

Adie heard no reaction from her friend. Timidly, she raised her face, and at that moment he erupted into uncontrollable laughter.

Adie felt hurt and tears even welled up in her eyes, "I expected sympathy, not mockery!" She could hardly speak and her voice was trembling.

Her friend seemed to be trying hard, but he couldn't stop laughing. "Sorry, Adie, but you are really very silly." He laughed again, adding, "As silly... as silly... as only a genius can be!"

Adie just frowned. She still didn't understand.

Eventually her friend's laughter subsided, and he explained, "157 is the IQ of a genius. They don't even count the scores above 130+. So, my darling, you are not just very smart, you're so intelligent that I feel humbled to be in your company, in the presence of a genius."

Adie stared at her friend in disbelief. He was being serious. She started to fumble desperately in her pockets, found a handkerchief, and pulled it out to wipe her eyes and blow her nose. She sipped from her glass of juice, made herself comfortable on her chair, then a smile lit up her face. "Really?" She clapped her hands and screamed, "Oh wow! How silly I am!" which made them both burst into laughter.

Since that day, several years had passed but Adie was still regularly receiving offers of free tests. She always deleted them, but today's offer promised to reveal her vocation. Adie just couldn't resist such an offer.

"I'll do it quickly," she decided. "It won't take more than ten minutes," she thought as she clicked the link to the test. There were 71 questions to fill in. Adie entered her answers, then clicked 'Send'.

While somewhere in the world a machine was stirring up the results, preparing to reveal her destiny, Adie scratched her scalp. But this was no itch; it was a gesture of despair, indicating that, at this moment, things were just not under her control.

Within seconds a chart appeared on the screen, with a short text:

You are an INVENTOR.
Possible professions include: systems designer, venture capitalist, actor, journalist, investment broker, real estate agent, real estate developer, strategic planner, political manager, politician, special projects developer, literary agent, restaurant/bar owner, technical trainer, diversity manager, art director, personnel systems developer, computer analyst, logistics consultant, outplacement consultant, advertising creative director, radio/TV talk show host.

"What a lot of bullshit…" muttered Adie in her mind. She had already done many of the things listed. Some of them she had liked, others she knew she could do perfectly despite disliking them, but she knew for certain that none of them were her calling. The rest of the things listed she didn't even want to think about and hoped she would never have to try them.

Adie suddenly felt a deep regret that she had wasted time on this utter nonsense. She felt even more frustrated when she realized it had taken her 20 minutes, double the time expected. She swore to never take any tests again.

Adie scolded herself , "How can you continue behaving as if you have learned nothing over the last year, Aida! You won't find your vocation just from getting a computer to tell you what you already know! You won't find it if you continue pushing the potential up against the wall, throttling it, leveling a gun against it, pulling a knife on it… Now forget this bullshit and get on with some work!"

Adie angrily closed down her internet browser and began shuffling the files on her desk, searching for something that could still be done in the few remaining hours of her day. But her mind could not settle on her work. She was still thinking about the test and how she'd been mechanically fitted to a list of professions defined as 'her'. The process they offered had no connection with Adie, the unique human being with specific needs; it had nothing to do with her fundamental essence.

Adie recalled her thoughts from a few days ago, that she was probably not one but a multiple personality, and the discovery of last night that her sense of plurality probably came from the loss of her original identity. Maybe, thought Adie, this might be why psychologists and psychiatrists had such a low success rate, throughout the 500 plus different schools of thought. Maybe they all started from the wrong presumption?

They each tried to define "the archetype" of the person, then attempted to heal that "I" they saw on the surface. The real problem, however, more often lay at a much deeper, more fundamental level, suppressed under layer upon layer of masks imposed by the rules of society and the demands of others. That, Adie reasoned, is why people in general are so unhappy: most of them are taught their identity by others, and have yet to discover their essential selves.

Adie looked out the window; rain was starting to fall. She forgot about the files on her desk and re-opened her internet browser. "Can't work in the rain!" she thought, with a clear conscience. She knew that her efficiency quotient was very high; when she did work, she completed more than enough to make up for days like these. Adie had discovered that most of the others did not finish in one week what she often completed in one day.

She did not know exactly how to define what she wanted to find on the Internet, so she just entered 'calling' in the search box. The first page of results related primarily to a calling to God. This seemed reasonable, given that English speakers were mostly Western Christians with a deterministic doctrine. This lead to a belief in being called to a vocation chosen by God (God's will) rather than, like in the Eastern Orthodox Church, making one's own choices in life as an act of human free will.

There was, however, a reference to a free-to-download book and Adie decided to check it out. The author promised to reveal techniques that would help anyone not only find a meaningful vocation, but also achieve it in practice.

Adie quickly downloaded the book and started reading. In the first chapter, the author wrote that no person was limited to only one calling and there was nothing wrong in having several. "Ha! Very interesting!" thought Adie, and her curiosity grew. She read on impatiently, eager to get to the promised techniques.

Soon she reached the page with instructions for the first exercise. Adie had to describe herself from the point of view of her favourite colour. The author stressed that she should pick her current favourite colour, on another day it could be a completely different colour. "Bravo!" Adie liked that. "We have free will over colours. Great start!"

Adie thought. In general, her favourite colour was green, but right now she felt blue. She began to write. "I'm blue. I am deep and calm, wise and cheerful. Life is born in me, that's why I am passionate, but I also radiate a tender coolness…"

Adie then read the author's comments and realised that he had tricked her into describing herself in a manner she would never normally do. Clearly the author knew many readers wouldn't freely describe themselves positively; it's more the norm to mention our defects.

Pleased with the first exercise, Adie moved on to the next, which asked her to mark as true or false a series of statements related to her childhood and the way her parents had treated her in the formative years of her personality. Though slightly suspicious about where this might lead, Adie completed the exercise.

About half the statements were true for her. There then followed claims about how parents can mess up their children's lives if they don't support sufficiently the first signs of what the child demonstrates as talents, interests and special gifts.

"Blah-blah… The inevitable bullshit!" Adie thought to herself, a little disappointed.

Her own parents had mostly supported the talents and interests that they saw emerging from her, even when it seemed impractical or when they thought her head was flying in the clouds. Basically, they had let her do what she liked and Adie greatly appreciated their supportiveness. But she did not believe that parents' influences should earn them blame for the way their child developed.

It beggared her belief whenever she heard someone speak of their 'childhood trauma'. Yes, environment was important, but who was to know how it might actually influence a child? It could take unpredictable directions. To some children, lack of support would be the motivation to accomplish their dreams, while others, even if they received all the support in the world, would do nothing, not even daydream.

The next exercise in the book required her to recall the first thing she had wanted to be when she grew up. The writer considered that this could very likely be a person's true vocation.

Adie remembered easily, as if it had been yesterday. As a 5-year-old girl she had loved to read. Her favourite book, Pippi Longstocking, she knew by heart, and Adie wanted exactly what Pippi wanted: to never grow up.

She even once asked her grandfather to go to the pharmacy for the chililug pills that Pippi and her friends Tommy and Annika took at the end of the book to remain as kids forever. Her grandfather just laughed a lot, but Adie never understood whether his laughter was a response to her question or not. At the time he had been reading The Adventures Of The Good Soldier Shveyk, so he was constantly giggling anyway.

Adie read on... the author explained that if the reader could not remember what they wanted to be when they grew up, then the other option was to remember what they had loved doing most as a child. Adie could not forget that either. She had loved to take out of the side drawer the big chocolate box that was filled with colourful buttons of every type and size, and tip them all out onto the big kitchen table. She would then bring them to life, imagining this one to be a princess, that one a ballerina; these would be an officer and his soldiers. Adie would imagine endless characters and weave them into fascinating stories. Left alone, Adie would be deeply absorbed in this game for hours.

Right now, however, she could make no connection between those buttons and her calling. Adie decided to come back to that puzzle and move on to the next exercise: to imagine in detail one perfect day, a day on which she had already found and was engaged in her calling. The author gave several examples, but Adie felt downhearted. "How can I describe my ideal day in which I do what I really want to do, when I do not know what I want to do?"

She noticed that in the given examples no one had escaped the routine patterns of their lives. The biggest difference that Adie could see was that in their ideal life some people slept in later.

Adie absolutely refused to waste time on such an exercise. She scrolled down to the second part of the book which promised to reveal the techniques that would enable the reader to implement their calling in real life (assuming that they had found what this was using the exercises in the first part of the book).

Adie was drawn to some interesting looking graphs and charts. They turned out to be step by step depictions of a production model used in the automotive industry.

"Brilliant!" thought Adie, with frustrated sarcasm. "Maybe the next exercise will show me how to put finding my calling on autopilot!"

Adie closed the book. "You begun well, lady," she addressed its author, "but unfortunately you ran out of imagination!" Then she sunk into her own thoughts, "Perhaps a vocation is the missing link ... the only thing ... that enables us to integrate the different personalities within ourselves. That's why it is so hard to find, because it has to appeal to the whole mob of personalities within us! For sure, I am not going to find it today." There was no time left to do any work, so she prepared to leave.

The rain had stopped and it had gone cold, but it was also very fresh, if a little sad somehow.

Adie wanted very much to talk to Alexey. She had felt so refreshed in the morning, but now, at the end of the same day she felt stuck and very lonely again. Yesterday, the world had embraced her with its beauty and had made her feel part of the magic of existence. Today, all of that was falling away from her, leaving her feeling like a stranger standing in the doorway, begging for shelter.

Adie walked slowly down Magic Alley, breathing the fresh air, but it gave no cheer to her soul. She found Lost In Paradise on her mp3 player, one of her favourite melodies by Armik[12]. At that moment, it touched her profoundly. "It's as if this guy is using my soul instead of a guitar," Adie thought. The music reflected every nuance of emotion she was feeling, the emotions of someone who knew that she was in heaven, but could not find the place appointed to her.

Adie pressed the repeat button when the melody finished. She would always listen over and over to any piece of music that matched her mood. Right now, it wasn't a smart thing to do, as by doing so, she was anchoring a feeling that was not good. She was saved by the ringing of her phone. It was Alexey who dragged Adie out of her trance.

[12]ARMIK - an Iranian-Armenian flamenco guitarist and composer.

"How did you know I wanted to talk to you?" Adie asked, without even greeting him. She wandered off the paving, waded in the grass and stopped under a pine tree. No one was around.

"Ah… is that you, Adie?" Alexey sounded surprised that it was. Then a smile entered his voice, "Well, I didn't know that I knew, but obviously I must have felt it," he answered to her question. "I was actually calling somebody else but I obviously I have dialed your number. Tell me, what's going on?"

"It's about me," Adie started. "I do not know. I just can't handle things. Just when I feel like I have climbed out of the shit, I slide back in again. I feel like… it's like I'm … lost in paradise." Adie instantly remembered that was the name of the melody she had just been listening to. "I feel so good, yet at the same time confused. I wander around admiring the wonder of everything in existence, but it also makes me terribly sad because I feel like I am not a part of it. I just can't bear this any more! I will explode! Who the hell am…"

"And I flutter with wings," Alexey interrupted her tirade.

"Pardon?" Adie asked, bewildered.

"This is your phrase," Alexey explained. "It's is a very powerful technique. By incorporating an absurd phrase into a problem, you break the mould in which you are stuck. And you seem to be stuck, from what I can hear…"

"And how did you come up with that phrase?" Adie demanded.

"I don't know. It came to me spontaneously. When you mentioned paradise, I saw angels fluttering around, although apparently you see devils!" Alexey laughed.

"Very funny, indeed!" Adie said, faking offence in her tone, but she had to laugh too as she asked, "What shall I do with this phrase?"

"Just repeat what you have already said to me, but when I say 'and' you will immediately say 'and I flutter with wings'," explained Alexey.

"OK," Adie agreed and began. "I do not know what happens but I can't handle…"

"And!" cried Alexey.

"... and I flutter with wings ... and just when it seems as if I have climbed out of the shit..."

"And!"

"... and I flutter with wings ... and again I slide back into the shit. I feel like I am lost in paradise..."

"And!"

"... and I flutter with wings and I feel so good..."

"And!"

"... and I flutter with wings and at the same time I am so confused..."

"And!"

"... and I flutter with wings and I wander around..."

"And!"

"... and I flutter with wings and I admire the wonder of everything in existence..."

"And!" Alexey was relentless.

"... and I flutter with wings. And I can't bear this anymore. I will explode, but I will explode with laughter," and Adie did, almost neighing!

Alexey was also laughing. "OK, that's enough," he managed to say. "If you get stuck again, just repeat this phrase!"

"Thanks for cheering me up," Adie purred.

"You're welcome," Alexey assured her. They spoke some more to arrange a meeting about their project, and the conversation ended with, "...and I flutter with wings!"

Adie repeated the phrase to herself, smiling. Then she saw her bus coming and ran to catch it. She came home much more relaxed. Prior to sleep, she repeated to herself again, "And I flutter with wings."

10. CHAPTER TEN

In the morning, Adie woke very early. She tried unsuccessfully to return to her sleep. Suddenly she sneezed. Then again. With the third sneeze she realised she had entered one of her sneezing spasms, which meant at least seven or eight more sneezes that would also become increasingly loud.

Adie quickly slid out of bed, grabbing her clothes on the way as she dashed to the kitchen. She didn't want to wake her partner. It annoyed her to have to get up so early, with nearly an hour to go before the wake-up alarm. On the other hand she loved the quiet stillness of early morning, with no one to disturb her thoughts as she slowly sipped her coffee.

When she had finished sneezing, Adie turned the radio on. The last chords of a song was playing, with an intensely sad, heart-rending beauty. 'Splendid!' She thought in admiration. After the final note, an interview with the singer followed. She was a Fado singer, as Adie understood, listening carefully to what she was saying. In spite of the simultaneous translation, she could hear the language the singer spoke and sung a while ago. It was Portuguese.

Her speech sounded just as the song itself - both gentle and strong, with dramatic longing and subdued sadness and it was very beautiful to listen to. "If someone were to declare his love for me in that language I wouldn't let him stop!" Adie thought.

The radio host asked the singer how long she had been singing and what music meant to her. Adie strained her ears to hear the answer.

"I don't remember my first toy - if it was a doll or a truck but I remember very well the first Fado song that I heard. I can never forget, the memory is clear as if it was yesterday. Fado is my destiny, my life... My music is everything to me," the singer confessed.

Adie felt sad. 'It seems the world is full of people who have found their vocation and their life is complete and meaningful, unlike mine! I also don't remember if my first toy was a doll or a truck...' Adie tried to go back in time. 'Well... I remember the first book I read... And that since then I've adored books... but can reading books be a vocation?' she asked herself, provoked by the singer's disclosure.

They played another song of the singer's. It was very evocative, and the Portuguese language added its own specific charm. 'I'll download some Fado music for my mp3 player,' Adie decided. Her beloved partner had left the 'gadget' in the kitchen – that's how Adie called the device she always forgot the name of. It was like a miniature computer on which she could use the Internet. Adie switched it on and while she was still listening to the song, she wrote 'Fado' in the search box. Many links appeared.

At the beginning of the page she saw a reference to an article and opened it. Only when she started reading, Adie realized that Fado actually meant 'fate', 'destiny'. She shook her head in a manner of saying, "You should have guessed it," as she was somewhat familiar with the language. She also found that this musical style was closely related to her favourite word in Portuguese: '*saudade*'. This word didn't have an equivalent in any of the languages she had any idea about. Actually it was not so much a word but more a verbal mood. *Saudade* expressed in a unique way the nostalgic longing for something that had been lost or didn't even exist. It was a vague and constant feeling of an absence, accompanied by intense, constant and emotionally devastating yearning and love for what was missing.

'Well, today 'the one above' just surpassed himself!' Adie exclaimed to herself. 'Hey, you've chosen a unique way to describe how I feel' she turned now directly to her top friend.

"And now Frank Sinatra and *My way*," announced the voice from the radio.

"Hm!" Adie reacted, this time aloud, and let the song take her attention. It was one of her favorite – she was always moved when she was listening to it.

For what is man, what has he got?

If not himself, then he has naught

She had always accepted this verse as wise words but now she saw a special message to her.

'I have to find it…It's somewhere here, buried in me… The answer is in me,' Adie said to herself. The song finished and she checked the clock. It was time to get ready for work.

When she arrived at the office, she found her desk was covered by a huge pile of letters, requests for samples of a product. Adie had to log each one on the computer. She started immediately, knowing that this would take all day and there would be no help. Since it was purely mechanical and required little thought, Adie realised she could make it more enjoyable by listening to music at the same time. She thought she needed that compensation for the injury. To Adie, any activity that numbed her mind was an injury.

Despite the music, by the end of the day Adie felt frazzled by this activity which should have been done by her technical assistant. If she had one. Irritated that she had to do work for a whole team, Adie thought this was the perfect moment to ask her boss for a pay raise.

Without a moment's thought, she dialed her manager's extension to see if he was available right now. The line was free, but when she heard the signal, she suddenly changed her mind. Thinking it might be better to wait until she was in a better frame of mind she hung up and tapped the desk thoughtfully.

'Why not write it down first… so I don't miss anything out… She considered her reasons then immediately opened a new file and started writing:

Dear Boss,
I'd like to have a chat with you, one that I've been meaning to have with you for a long time.

While she was wondering how to continue, a voice inside her head surprisingly said out of nowhere: *'The key is under the mat'*. 'What does that mean? Sounds familiar,' Adie was at a loss. 'Oh, yes!' she remembered suddenly and smiled. Once, worried whether her salary would last the month, she tried a new technique from the seminar. This involved explaining one's problem in such a way that it was completely incomprehensible; what's more, it should have no rational logic and be embellished with absurd details. The nonsense retelling should continue until a word or a phrase came up, which the narrator recognized as a key one. Then he should use the key in some way: repeat it or put it in a poem, sing it, act it out… all sorts of creative interpretations were possible.

On one occasion, when she just handed over her last banknote in the supermarket, Adie had decided to try the technique. Dumping her shopping onto the kitchen table she took out the little notebook from the pile of her dear one's newspapers and, still standing, began writing whatever came into her mind:

The hen made a drawing of a window and poked its head out to spit, but the cloth hit it on the neck and it flew down to the gaping mouth of the krontosaurus, which was yawning, and when it passed by the third floor, a sock shouted at it: 'The key is under the mat!

Adie smiled. 'Well done! That was actually quite easy,' she congratulated herself, recognizing her phrase. She didn't need to write any further and started singing: 'The key is under the mat, the key is under the mat,' while putting away her shopping. Still singing while changing her clothes, she remembered she still kept their small, old postbox key in her purse; she took it out, opened the door and placed it gently under the doormat.

A little later, a friend called to ask Adie if they could meet up the next day because she wanted to give back some money Adie had lent her. Adie had completely forgotten about that.

So now, when this same phrase came to mind while writing to her boss, Adie thought, "That's no accident." After short reflection, she decided to insert it in the letter, among the sentences; the same way Alexey had put 'And I flutter my wings' into her problem narration the other day.

Adie added *'The key is under the mat,'* after *'Dear boss, I've been considering having this conversation with you for a long time already'* and continued writing:

I don't think that I've been bothering you with any personal claims over all these years – I don't even remember to have ever wanted anything because …

Adie thought about 'why' and heard the answer in her head '…because the key is under the mat.' She smiled and felt the muse was welling up:

Actually, I've always been modest like this and I've never demanded a thing… Even when people asked me if I wanted chocolate or anything I loved I used to say 'no, thank you'...

The serious intention to ask for a pay raise was turning into a parody and Adie started enjoying it a lot. Somehow her resentment had gone away. 'So much the better', she said to herself. In the next moment she was totally engrossed in the letter, and a smile was blossoming on her face.

... Anyway, the key is under the mat and I won't bother you with my childhood traumas.

Adie could hardly stifle her giggling.

I hope (she continued rattling quickly on the keyboard), you know how good I am and that I work quietly here in my corner, for which the key is under the mat... And despite all you have inflicted on me, which added to childhood traumas could kill even a mare, I still love you... And yet, boss, you must remember that the key is under the mat and that everything has a limit...

'What nonsense!' Adie exclaimed to herself and continued inspired:

I know that my love does not matter to you and that's why I don't ask you to requite it. What I ask is just money and I believe this is quite a relief for you, having in mind that, the key is under the mat and you will have to pay for the cheese...

'This letter is a real tommy-rot,' Adie thought smiling and decided to end the merry-making here.

Maybe, boss, you often stay awake at night, wondering why the key is under the mat...? Sorry, but I won't make it easy for you and I'll leave it to you to find out...

The working day was over. While Adie's colleagues were beginning to leave, she reread her letter, delighted with its spontaneity. Having written such a masterpiece, she was determined it reach her boss.

She was going to sign it, but decided it would be better to leave the letter anonymous. At first she thought to e-mail it but realized it was easy to track back the sender and dropped the idea. In a while a better one occurred. She selected the text and changed the font color from black to white. The document on the screen appeared completely white. Adie waited for her colleagues to go out and printed the letter – the sheet that came out of the printer seemed empty. 'Yes, but it isn't,' Adie thought contentedly. She looked out of the window and couldn't see her boss' car; he had already left. She took the letter, opened the office door and listened; the coast was clear. In the corridor, she tiptoed as quickly as she could to her boss's office, crouched in front of the door and slipped the letter through the gap below.

'Tomorrow, when he enters he'll pick it up and 'read' it" – she thought. She imagined her boss unlocking the door, taking a few steps, then bending and picking the sheet up off the floor. Then, he would look at it without seeing anything; he'd turn it over and be just as puzzled. He would shrug his shoulders and put it on his desk…

'It doesn't matter how, the letter will fall into his hands,' Adie was sure about it. She stood up, again rushed back to her office on tiptoes, and quickly went in. She was so amused with what she had done, that she started whistling her favourite horo[13] and danced few steps in the middle of the office before someone knocked on her door. She quickly put on a professional face and opened it to find the security guard. When he enquired as to whether she was leaving soon, she nodded and mentally gave thanks that he hadn't arrived a minute earlier.

To her astonishment, one morning, about ten days after she had written the letter, her boss rang her up. When she entered his office, Adie noticed that he looked tired. He asked her if she was fine and when she said she was great, he began to complain that for some time he hadn't been able to sleep well. Then he praised the work she'd done lately and said there was a small cash bonus for her. Adie thanked him politely and on leaving the office, she looked in the envelope that he gave her.

It really was a "small" cash bonus. "Don't worry you can't afford anything more now, boss. You already know that the key is under the mat, don't you? So, use it often, boss. You can even carry it with you, if you want, as a boss-collar! And sleep well!" Adie mentally spoke to her boss, laughed, put the money in her pocket and headed off to her office.

She enjoyed the fresh air as she strolled slowly along her Magic Alley. Her phone rang; it was a friend she hadn't seen for ages. She happened to be in the area where Adie lived and wanted to go for a cup of coffee. Adie rejoiced at the opportunity and they arranged to meet in twenty minutes at the bus station.

[13] "Horo" is a typical Bulgarian chain folk dance, that often has the unique in music worldwide uneven, asymmetric rhythm.

Adie hurried to catch the bus. After a short ride, she saw her friend already there, waiting. They hugged each other and set out for the nearest pub to celebrate their serendipitous reunion with some wine. It turned out that Adie's friend was around for a job interview.

Adie really liked her friend. She thought of her as a very decent woman, pleasant, intelligent, humorous… but this lovely woman was still alone, or at least she had been last time Adie had seen her. She couldn't find love. Adie asked if there had been any change in that department.

"No," replied her friend, obviously tortured by the fact. "It seems impossible for me to find the right man; and my biological clock is not slowing down."

Adie did not want to dwell on the subject. She did not know what to say to help. She began telling her friend about the seminars with Alexey. Then suddenly stopped and squinted at her friend, "Do you have the ad with you for the job you've applied for?"

"Yes … Why?"

"Give it to me, please!" Adie held out her hand.

Her friend rummaged in her bag and pulled out a neatly folded sheet on which she had printed the job advert from the Internet. She handed it over, curious about Adie's intentions.

"This will help explain what I've been up to, lately." Adie unfolded the paper and quickly read the ad. Her eyes brightened, "This is exactly what I need!"

Adie took out the notebook and pen that were always in her bag and laid them in front of her friend. "We will place an ad for your man!" Adie smiled. Her friend looked bewildered.

"You see, my dear," Adie began to explain, citing Alexey, "for something to happen, you must *let* it happen. And to let it happen, you need to take the seriousness out of it. You are taking this situation so seriously that you are blocking all the possibilities for what you want to happen in your life."

"Well, of course I take it seriously," insisted her friend. "I have to. It is serious. How can it happen if I am not serious about it?"

"On the contrary," Adie continued, "You have just got used to thinking that you must take seriously the things you see as important in your life."

"So what should I do, make a joke of them?"

"Wouldn't harm you!" Adie teased.

"I don't get you," admitted her friend.

"No need to," Adie smiled. "You may not understand now, but please do what I am going to suggest to you. Just try and let's see what happens."

"Well, I'm listening," agreed her friend.

Adie began to give her instructions. "Read through the job ad and rewrite it as if you are the company seeking an employee, who in this case is your ideal man. Here… see where it says that the company is a leader in its field? Write your name and present yourself as *a most pleasant and beautiful woman, well-known for her intelligence, charm, good humour, passion, kindness…*' Put whatever you want about yourself, and do not skimp on the superlatives!"

Adie's friend was smiling now. She had begun to grasp the idea. And she liked it.

"Then here…" continued Adie, "where they specify what they were looking for, you write *HUSBAND*." Her friend was now laughing loudly. "Come on, begin writing!" urged Adie.

The woman wrote as instructed, coping with the task quite quickly.

"Now, you determine what the requirements for the job are. Let's say, '*university degree in economics*' can become '*well developed personality*', and '*experience in a similar position an advantage*' can become '*experience in successful male-female relationships an advantage*'. Unless, of course, you want someone who has never touched a woman in his life," Adie added with a smile.

She continued, "You have to be clear about your requirements and you have to be specific. And only use positive expressions. For example, say '*must be a teetotaller*' rather than '*must not drink heavily*'. It's a peculiar thing, isn't it? The world doesn't seem to accept the 'not'. Nor does your subconscious mind.

"How so?" asked the friend.

"Well …" Adie recalled the time Alexey had explained it to her. "Think of no orange squirrel…" she suggested. "What did you think of?"

"An orange squirrel," the woman answered.

"That's what I mean, you see? Your brain didn't register the word 'no' and showed you an orange squirrel. If you want a squirrel that isn't orange you have to tell your brain exactly what kind of squirrel you want, using positive language. This same principle operates on a wider scale. Do you understand?"

"Yes," nodded her friend.

"And another very important factor," Adie went on, "is to focus not on the form but on the essence."

Her friend sighed. "You've lost me again," she said, frowning.

"There was a woman, who really wanted to find a man," Adie explained, "just like you do. She imagined him in her mind: tall, slim, blue eyes, black hair… One day, browsing through a magazine, she saw a picture of a man much like the one she'd imagined. She cut out the picture and pinned it to the visualisation board on her bedroom wall, where she would see it frequently. The idea was to make him materialise by keeping the picture in her mind. Well, she soon met a man very similar to the one in the picture, and it led to a relationship.

"But it didn't last long. The man turned out to be an alcoholic. Things rapidly went downhill. With a broken heart, she decided to remove the image from her wall; it was painful to be reminded of him. As she looked at the picture for the last time, she noticed that the man was holding a glass in his hand; the picture had come from an advert for alcohol. This had escaped her attention previously; she had only seen the man's physical features, not focussed at all on the essence of the person she would like to share her life with. I read this in a book. I don't know, but I'm inclined to believe it is true," Adie concluded.

"I see," said her friend.

Adie had yet more instructions. "And another thing you must

remember..."

"Gosh! Will you never stop!" her friend interrupted with a smile.

Adie was unperturbed, "This should be fun. If at any point you feel that you are taking it too seriously, just drop it."

"Sure," the woman was happy to accept this instruction.

"OK, then. You can finish this at home. Don't forget the part where it says what the company offers: *'attractive remuneration package with additional benefits'* can become *'attractive remuneration package with love and respect, and additional bonuses such as occasional cooking and laundry'* ...*and lots of sex!"* Both of them laughed. "Just have fun," Adie repeated. "Oh, and make sure you include an address where the applications should be sent."

"Are you serious?" the friend was not so sure about that part.

"Absolutely!" insisted Adie, "How else is the guy supposed to find you? But you need not use your real address; it could be something like *The Head of Heart Issues at The Department Of Emotional Affairs.*"

"And what do I do with the ad after I've written it?" asked the friend.

"Publish it!" Adie was adamant.

"No way!" her friend was equally resistant.

"I don't mean really do it," laughed Adie. "All of this is a parody. We want to release some tension from the situation, not screw it up tighter." Adie thought a moment. "To publish your announcement, you could make a wall of your bedroom the notice board of your company and put your ad up there. Or buy a newspaper and staple your ad into the Jobs section. Improvise!"

"Well, I can do that," said her friend with relief, "and shall I add a deadline for applying?"

Adie thought for a moment. "Yes!" she decided emphatically. "And make it absurdly short ...three days from tomorrow."

"Why so short?"
"To avoid creating expectations. These things seem to work better when

they stretch our belief. I think that after thirty years without the right man it'll be tough for you to believe that he could show up in a mere three days?"

Adie explained further. "If you gave yourself a month, then during that month you'd start to count the days, wanting each day to be the day. It's the trap of expectation. You would only get more disappointed as each day turned out to be not the day. And that feeling of disappointment would become a barrier.

"I understand," said the friend, "but what if it doesn't happen in three days?"

"Who says it won't happen in three days?" Adie asked, and immediately answered, "Only your own brain says so." She looked at her watch. It was time to leave, there was nothing for dinner at home and she hadn't warned her partner that she would be late. Adie and her friend hugged as they left the pub, and promised each other that they should meet up more often.

"You call me if something happens!" Adie insisted as they parted.

"Sure!" promised her friend.

On her way home, Adie thought deeply. "Maybe I should place an advert too … for my calling".

After a week, Adie's friend phoned to report that three days had definitely passed but no candidate had come forward for the vacant position.

"Quite the contrary," countered Adie. "It is for you to decide that he has applied. And not just anyone, but the ideal candidate. Once you have done that, all that remains is to appoint him to the position."

"What are you talking about, Adie?" Her friend was confused.

Adie was thinking of an example Alexey had given, of a woman who was also searching for a partner. Alexey had told her that what she needed to do was allow the man to come into her life. He had instructed her to buy a pair of men's slippers and put them at 'his side' of her bed.

It had worked for that woman, and Adie decided it would also work for her friend. "Buy something," she instructed her, that will make you feel there is a man living in your house, like slippers, and put them on his side of your bed. And put some shaving things in the bathroom. Make it as if he is already a part of the team."

"Rather crazy!" commented her friend.

"What's crazy is not being able to find your man for so many years!" Adie reacted rather sharply. She forgot that not everyone attended seminars led by Alexey, that this was all new to them and a lot to take on board.

The woman remained silent.

"Sorry," Adie relented. "I didn't mean to criticise or blame you. I just want to explain how there is more than one way for these things to happen. We don't even try some of the ways because someone else has branded them as "crazy". I'd really like to meet the wise sage who has defined normal. I don't see why we should limit ourselves. I think that what is normal is quite flexible and something we should always be expanding…" Adie ran out of breath from her hurried apology.

The woman was still silent.

"Listen," Adie tried a different approach, "if you don't like the idea, don't do it. You should only do this if you like it."

"Adie, I do like the idea. I even got a little excited imagining his slippers on his side of my bed. But this is all so different from anything I've done before, so different that…" she struggled for a word, "It's not normal for me!"

Relieved she had not offended her friend, Adie made a suggestion. "How about you ask some guy from your office to take his socks off and give them to you at the end of the workday. Then you can drop them in the middle of the bedroom, just like guys do. Make it more authentic, even with "a scent of a man"!"

Both friends erupted into laughter.

Adie didn't hear from her friend for the next three months. Adie often thought about giving her a call but something else always seemed to crop up. Then, out of the blue, her friend phoned. Adie immediately sensed something different in her tone of voice; as if it was carrying a happy smile.

Her friend was calling to invite Adie to her wedding.

Adie listened to an unbroken stream of accolades about her friend's husband-to-be. She had met him about a week after last speaking with Adie. After that phone call, she had bought a pair of men's socks, and had dropped them carelessly next to the slippers on his side of the bed. And now, she couldn't help but giggle every night when she saw him doing the same.

"Isn't marriage a little sudden?" cautioned Adie.

"Not at all!" her friend reassured her. "Things have evolved really quickly. In fact, there's a good reason for the rush … I'm pregnant!"

"Oh!" shrieked Adie with enthusiasm. "An unexpected side-effect!"

"Adie…" the woman adjusted herself to serious mode, "I don't know if all those shenanigans you led me on have anything to do with what has happened in my life … but … thank you!"

"You are welcome," Adie smiled, "but it was you that did it, I haven't done anything. If you get stuck in any situation again, you now know how to get yourself out."

They talked some more, and Adie promised to come to the wedding.

After dinner that night, her partner got lost in a football match on TV. That was not a problem for Adie. He could waste his time if he wished; she had something important to do. But she sat with her back towards him, so that her quiet laughter would not attract his curiosity while she created her advertisement for her calling.

The AIDA group of companies includes many personalities commanding a large share of the market in fast-moving opportunities and ideas. Due to rapid growth over the past year, AIDA now has an urgent requirement for a proven professional to take up the vacant position of

CALLING

The ideal candidate must be
- available 24 hours a day 7 days a week
- to satisfy the needs of the company in any way required with complete loyalty
- able to adapt quickly to a dynamic environment
- able to show clear evidence of meeting all requirements for this position

Previous experience in a similar position will be an advantage.

The company offers
- opportunities for lifelong development
- a close working relationship with the management
- a prestigious office on the top floor of the company HQ reflecting the importance of
  this position
- copious levels of gratitude linked to performance
- special treatment and many other bonuses

All applications will be treated with strict confidentiality. Short-listed candidates will
be appointed on probation for three days.

Send CV and covering letter to:

Special Needs Manager
Department of Human Resources
AIDA

ALL APPLICATIONS
MUST BE SUBMITTED IMMEDIATELY

Adie dabbed faint tears of laughter from her cheeks. As finding her vocation was of such vital importance, she decided to send the message to the Universe in a more dramatic way. She rolled up the advertisement, tied it up with a red woolen thread, put it in a small plastic bottle and went to the bathroom, where she poured some water into the basin and dropped the bottle there to float, confident that the SOS message would go to the right place.

Satisfied with her efforts, Adie remembered Alexey had asked the group to prepare a doll for the next seminar, which was to be about label removal. They were going to explore removing from themselves the labels that had been attached to them, by society or maybe even by themselves. The doll they had to make was supposed to represent the packaging of their personality in a social form that obscured their true nature.

Adie was not very skilled in handicrafts, but surprised herself by quickly creating a doll that was rather good. At least she thought so. After just twenty minutes or so, her rag-doll was ready.

As a finishing touch, Adie stuck a face onto the doll, cut out from a photo of herself. She chose a rather ugly photo in which she did not look at all happy. Alexey had emphasised that the puppet was to serve as a reminder of themselves as a social entity. "As a social being, I'm unhappy," Adie thought as she glued her face into its place on her ragged creation.

All that remained was to name the doll. The name of the doll had to be different from that of the person represented by it, yet it still had to be somehow related to that person.

Adie named her doll Princess. As a schoolgirl, she used to tell everyone that her great grandfather had been a king. She had even inscribed her school notebooks with the name Princess.

Adie went to bed in a happy frame of mind, taking her newly born puppet with her as she slipped under the covers with a long sigh of contentment. When her partner noticed the intruder in their bed, he made his usual swirling hand gesture which meant, "I think you are completely crazy." He looked intently at her, expecting some explanation.

"I will explain it to you some other time," was all that Adie offered. Her eyelids were already feeling weighty. She popped her Princess under her pillow, turned onto her stomach and fell asleep immediately.

11. CHAPTER ELEVEN

In the morning, Adie got out of bed with her doll and put it immediately in her bag, so she didn't forget it. She got ready for work quickly and arrived at the office before her colleagues. Except for a fifteen minute lunch break, she worked non-stop right through to the end of the day. "Now I can doze for the rest of the month," she thought, pleased with herself for the amount of work that she had completed.

After work, Adie had about 40 minutes, plenty of time, before the meeting with Alexey. A bus came almost immediately, but at the first major junction it was blocked by a traffic jam.

Just as Adie started to worry that she would be late, she heard the voice of Alexey in her head, "Such transport constipation!" He had said this one time before, when they were in a taxi caught up in a similar traffic jam. It had made her laugh then, and she could barely hold back her laughter now. She tried, but the result sounded like a series of little grunts. She immediately clasped her hands over her nose and mouth, pretending to have sneezed.

She felt like laughing even more. The giggles took over and she found it hard to stop until the bus arrived at the stop she had to change at. Making her way off the bus, past glances from several people who had obviously decided she was one of those you often see on public transport who were 'not all there'. To Adie, these people had the same problem as the traffic.

"Transport constipation!" She still couldn't resist laughing out loud now, as she hopped off the bus, just making her connection. She arrived on time, even shortly before Alexey, for their pre-seminar meeting.

"I have so many things to tell you," Adie began, before Alexey was even in his seat.

"Then tell me," he encouraged her.

She hesitated, unsure where to begin, then chose to describe the 'therapy' she had proffered her soon-to-be-married friend.

"Brilliant reframing, Adie. Just brilliant!" Alexey praised her. "You used powerful metaphors that wouldn't even have occurred to me. You should try working with real clients!"

"No, I won't practice therapy," Adie resisted.

"Why not? You do it so well." Alexey was surprised.

"But it's just not my calling. I *do* enjoy doing it, sometimes; it's like being a muse. But I can't do it like that with people who are expecting answers there and then."

Alexey remained silent, as if disappointed that Adie did not want to practice.

Adie broke the silence. "What will we need to do next for our project?"

She was referring to the project she had convinced Alexey that they should start soon: to acquaint a wider audience with his approach. She believed it could be used by anyone, without the need to have studied psychology.

Adie had brought to Alexey's notice that the seminar was now being attended by more people who had nothing to do with psychology, while many of the academic psychologists had dropped out. It seemed they could not, or simply would not, abandon their frameworks of theoretical constructs that had been jammed into their heads.

In Alexey's approach, there were no complex theories, not even simple ones. On the contrary, the process was inherent within human nature. Anyone could be shown how to make it work for themselves and become creators of their own destiny.

But right now, Adie's thoughts were not really on the project. Alexey's poignant silence seemed to be insisting on a direct answer. There had been a time when Adie did consider psychotherapy to be her calling; she had really made a difference to people's lives with truly remarkable results. But, as often happened when Adie was doing well at something, her passion for it at breakfast time was gone by lunch time, so to speak.

"I do want to do this, Alexey," Adie admitted, "but not in this way, not as a therapist. Rather, I want to have a role in somehow helping to make this available to all people, not just through individual sessions. I want to make it so that the ears of those who hear will listen, as the Bible says."

"I understand you," Alexey reassured her.

"That's why I suggested this project with you. People are interested! It's like, you know, better to teach a man how to fish rather than catching the fish for him and feeding it to him." Adie's voice began to strain with agitation, but she continued. "I feel that people these days are somehow more open-minded. Maybe it's because these days we are buried in information, so we have developed a new ability to sort it out for ourselves. I think it's important for people to learn how to use what they already have within themselves to make their own choices about the things outside of themselves." Adie paused.

"Right," Alexey encouraged her.

She continued with fervour. "Enough with all the ready-made recipe approaches. Even the smartest person will become stupid if they live only on what is prescribed for them. They could have God Himself as their personal psychotherapist, but even He won't be able to help them if they won't even think for themselves."

Next, Adie enlisted Alexey to her crusade. "You've said it yourself, that no matter how many explanations you give people, the most they can do with them is become specialists in explaining their problems. They won't find solutions, whatever the explanation might be."

Adie was now really firing up. "They have renounced their own lives and their freedom. They have renounced their duty as the 'crown of creation' made in the 'image and likeness of God', creators of their own reality. And that means they have to clean up their own shit instead of waiting for someone else to do it for them!"

Alexey laughed at her last words. This brought Adie back to earth and she laughed too. "I'm sorry. I'm getting into this now." Adie calmed her voice.

"No need to apologise; you put it perfectly," Alexey smiled. "Tonight, we shall deal with that."

"Cleaning up shit?" laughed Adie.

"Something like that," Alexey replied, also laughing.

Adie changed the topic. "Have you always wanted to be a psychologist?" she asked Alexey, surprised she had never asked him that before.

"No, I once thought that I wanted to be a pig farmer."

Adie giggled, "You are joking?"

"I'm serious," Alexey smiled, and told her how one day he'd decided he did not want to be a psychologist any more, and actually got himself a job looking after pigs. "But very quickly, I got sick of doing that all day and realised that what I wanted more than anything was to be a psychologist. So I abandoned the pigs."

With that, it was time to leave for the seminar. Adie sighed and thought, "I didn't manage to tell him everything, but next time, I will."

As usual, the others were already there at the seminar office, this time animatedly comparing each other's rag-doll creations. As they sat and calmed down, Alexey asked them to put their dolls aside for now, "Because today we're going to have fun and much laughter,"

"Great!" responded the group.

"First, we will look at a basic principle, an idea from new psychology, that will help us. In 1936, Korzhibski[14] said that 'the map is not the territory'. We all hold a mental map in our heads about what life is, how to live, who we are, what is possible, what is not possible and so on. This mental map determines our perception of the world, but what it shows us is not the world.
"We use our map just like geographic maps, to orient us in the territory

---

[14] Alfred Korzhibski (1879-1950) was a philosopher and scientist of Polish-American descent. He is mainly known for the theory of general semantics.

we find ourselves in, because the map makes the world understandable to us. This map, however, shows only a small piece of the territory, and it differs from person to person.

"With geographic maps, everything is clear and very specific. The city is here, there is a mountain, here is the sea, there the river... A mental map is much more complicated, and less clear. Parts of it can be unconscious, thus allowing or forbidding events in a person's life without their awareness.

"Let me first clarify something so that you won't be misled. By 'territory' we understand reality in general, and this reality has an interesting property. It is like when you pour liquid into a container: the liquid takes the form of the container. In the same way, reality flows into our maps, and thus our maps shape our reality.

"When we fill our mind with something, like a problem for example, then our mental map will take the shape of the problem. That is why for some people life is predominantly problematic, whereas for other people it is predominantly positive. Whatever the form of the container that they submit to reality, that's what reality fills up and it takes that form for them.

"Another concept now comes into view. It seems contradictory, but it really does follow that 'the territory is the map'. In other words, the mental map that we hold shapes our reality that we experience.

"Ultimately, we are not slaves to our map, especially not when we understand all this. Today's exercises are designed to show us that we can go beyond the limits of the reality that we have shaped."

Alexey paused.

"Well then, let's get going!" somebody said, taking advantage of the silence.

Alexey continued, regardless. "Often, people will tell me that they have lost a sense of meaning in their lives..."

On hearing this, Adie slid down her chair, as if trying to disappear under it, although she was sure that Alexey would not be talking about her personally.

"...For me, this is a sure sign that their map has begun to lead their life, instead of them leading it, and that this map has exhausted the meaning which it once had for them." Alexey paused again.

Adie felt that she had blushed. She could not help associating herself with what she had heard, and she did not like it. She felt stupid. She raised her hand to her head and began to scratch her scalp."

Alexey continued, "Whatever that meaning had once been … to fulfill responsibilities to their family, for example … at a certain point it appears that this map no longer reflects the person's real needs and wishes.

"The good thing here is that this existential crisis could serve as a redirection to this person, and as a way for them to get rid of it. It gives a signal that there are other directions and that the map should be changed. When that map is subjected to change, then reality responds to that change. Consequently, other things start to happen.

"Now, you should know that 'the map' is itself a whopping big label. I'm telling you this because we are now going to the un-labelling exercises that I mentioned earlier. We've chosen all sorts of labels for ourselves, and the map is our way of organising them. But, before proceeding to the exercises, let's see how a label works."

He paused only briefly before explaining, "The problem with labels is that they are very prescriptive, in fact they are a total prescription, not only for our behaviour but also for how to experience things and what to think. Through organising things, the label conquers them. If we can remove the label, we will find that we can be much freer in our actions, feelings and thinking.

"I'm not only talking about negative labels, like 'idiot' or 'silly cow', which we seem to bandy about so much these days. This also applies to positive labels such as 'good', 'intelligent', 'beautiful' and so on."

Alexey reached into his bag and pulled out a few sheets of bright yellow adhesive labels. "Let's have some fun now. For our first exercise, each of you is going to write a few labels, positive and negative, on these yellow notes. Then you will stick half of them on yourselves, and the rest on other people in the group."

Giggles erupted in anticipation of the potential fun that could follow, even before the dolls. Alexey gave out the yellow stickers and they all began writing.

Adie soon finished her negative labels: *'stubborn'*, *'lazy'* (to which she added 'in some things'), and '*selfish*' (which she again qualified with 'sometimes'). Her positive labels she struggled with, embarrassed at being too full of herself. She finally settled for '*clever*', then '*generous*' (to which she again added 'with some things'). She hesitated over her third positive label, unsure whether it was positive or negative. Finally, she decided that '*self-sufficient*' was positive for her, and wrote it down.

When everyone had written their labels, they began sticking them on themselves and others; on their faces, hands, clothes, feet... Tears of laughter began flowing as they pointed their fingers at each other. When everyone was covered with labels, Alexey, who had left the room, returned with a waste paper basket which he placed in the middle of the room. He told them to remove their labels now, one by one, to crush them and throw them into the basket. To make it more fun, they had to aim at the basket from a distance.

There was a new woman at this seminar. No one knew where she had learned about their meetings. On being instructed to bin her labels, she began collecting them from herself and from others, folding them very carefully and neatly. She even retrieved labels that had already been thrown away by others and smoothed them out for her collection. A number of blank looks were aimed at her.

"Throw them away!" Alexey repeated, "You don't need them; they're limiting you!"

"I won't throw them away!" The woman reacted sharply, and she continued foraging in the rubbish bin. What she found, she took with her back to her seat, collected her belongings, and left without saying a word.

The whole group was shocked by the woman's behaviour. "What was that?" someone asked.

"Some people," explained Alexey, "take their labels very seriously and do not want to get rid of them. To them, this is their life, their identity in the world, the map of their reality. They get scared when you try to take away their map; it would leave them in the middle of nowhere, naked in unfamiliar territory. That scares them. I'm used to seeing it, but if you're new to this it can be quite shocking."

Alexey shrugged. "Well, at worst she'll spread a rumour that some insane people gather here. Which is absolutely true, from her perspective. Let's continue."

For the next exercise, they had to write down some positive and negative labels in their notebooks. Then they had to sing out the labels with different melodies. That soon restored the group to bursts of crazy laughter.

Someone began to sing how intelligent, friendly, and well-organised he was, along with lots of other lovely qualities. But his tune was that of Beethoven's *Funeral March*. He followed that by praising his laziness, ugliness, malice and other repulsive features, using the tune of *Ode To Joy*.

To conclude this exercise, each of them had to choose the label they felt was the most powerful one for them, and act out a comic sketch on it.

After that, Alexey called a 5 minute break, so they could laugh to their hearts' content before moving on to the craziest part of the seminar ... the dolls.

After the break, Alexey asked them, one by one, to introduce their doll, their symbol of their social personality from the position of that personality. He first demonstrated with his own doll.

The next in line was Adie. "I'm a princess. I think I am so ...mmm ... princessy. And yet I can't even find my vocation! I always want to do great things, to prove something to myself and others, but I'm so lost that I don't know what I want to do and I have no idea how to find it. In a nutshell, I'm a silly cow with an IQ of 157..."

The whole group burst out laughing at that. Then, in turn, each of them presented their social packaging in the same style.

When all this was done, Alexey continued. "Now, you're going to deprive your social packaging of all the severity and seriousness it holds. Because it is the packaging that is the problem ... not you. In the essence of your being, you cannot have a problem.

"Now, when I give the signal, start tossing your dolls up into the air. And while they are up there, state your problem out loud. Keep on doing this until you get bored with it. At some point you'll feel something. Something will come to you: a sound, a word, a melody, an image... It can appear in your mind or you may notice it in the external environment. Whatever it is, this will be your mantra for this problem. For our purposes here, forget the common meaning of the word 'mantra'. We use it only to show that it is a special sign, one that you will use later whenever you think of or experience your problem. Now, everyone find a space and start throwing!"

Adie went into a corner and tossed her princess up in the air, repeating with each throw, "The princess has no vocation!" She continued for maybe five minutes before she was bored. She directed her attention within herself and, just as Alexey had promised, her mantra appeared. It was a word … *'Makumba'!*

It conveyed no meaning to her. When she told the group about it in the discussion that followed, someone remarked that it sounded rather African, but no one knew if there really was such a word.

"Do not seek logical explanations," Alexey warned. "It does not matter whether your mantra conveys any logical meaning or not. It is simply something that you recognise as yours. You do not need to make any correlations. If you do, it won't work. The connections here are of a different nature."

For the last exercise of the evening seminar, they were asked to express, in rhyme, a situation labeled by their social personality as a problem. They were to develop this situation from its negative state as a problem towards a positive direction.

There was silence while they all concentrated on poeticising. Adie remembered her recent experience, when she had been in a shitty mood and had tripped up in the dog turd. She remembered how that had made her laugh like crazy. She decided to take up the challenge to put this into a poem.

Everyone was finished surprisingly quickly. All that remained was for each of them to read out their literary efforts, the 'cherry' of this evening's seminar. Each poem was met with a storm of applause and laughter. This time, Adie came last in the line. She began to read:

In a shitty mood again
Awakens my Princess,
And she's starting to complain
Like a witch in dire distress.

Princess catches her bus
And, as if to give her honour,

She is greeted by a farting "Hissss!"
From some peasant squashed upon her.

Barely surviving this affront,
The call for her stop is heard,
But of her doom she must bear the brunt,
And she lands on a huge dog's turd.

Princess cannot handle this
So she returns to slumber.
Now Adie sees her shit-smeared Goddess
And her smirking laughter thunders.

Passers by witness and deplore
But much to their surprise,
Adie chuckles even more
As she starts to realize

Learn this lesson and have no fear,
Whatever comes to sight.
I'll make my message really clear:
Your myths make all your shite!

Loud applause followed. Several of her colleagues even asked Adie to give them a copy.

As the seminar that night had lasted longer than usual, Adie said her goodbyes quickly and left. On arriving home she found her dearest already having dinner. She joined him without bothering to change her clothes. Afterwards, she watched the film on TV, a predictable Hollywood romance, before taking her usual shower and retiring to bed.

Adie drifted off to sleep, softly repeating the mantra that had come to her while tossing her princess, "Makumba… Makumba…"

12. CHAPTER TWELVE

Her mobile phone rang. Adie read the large letters that displayed the caller's name:

VANGA[15]

Adie felt a shiver of intrigue trickle down her spine. The famous prophetess was calling her? The phone stopped ringing as she was about to answer. She hesitated, then pressed the key to call back the number.

A voice immediately answered, "I must tell you this. I will just explode if I don't tell you this!"

"Who is this?" Adie demanded to know, feeling let down that it was a male voice. "It said it was Vanga calling me." Clearly it was not.

The man ignored her and began to tell her a story, interrupted only by his own frequent reels of laughter, punctuated by hiccups. "My grandmother sneezed and her jaw flew off her mouth like a rocket … (laughter and hiccups) … It shot onto the floor and slid under the bed … (laughter) … She had to drag it out using her rolling pin because she could not reach it by hand … (hiccups) … Can you imagine, her arse sticking up in the air as she pulled out her jaw from under the bed? … (hiccups) … Actually, when she sneezed she had clenched her bladder so tight, so she

---

[15] Vanga (1911 –1996) was a blind Bulgarian woman-mystic, supposed clairvoyant and herbalist. Many people believe she possessed paranormal abilities.

wouldn't wet herself, because she had been desperate to pee ... (laughter) ... so her mouth opened instead of her bladder, and the force blew her jaw away ... (laughter and hiccups)..."

At this point, as she listened to this crazy story, Adie's smile broke into laughter too. Who on earth was this, using Vanga's phone to call her and tell her such nonsense? If it really was Vanga calling her, Adie would have expected it to be about something of crucial importance.

"Forget what came up on your mobile's display," said the male voice, as if he had read her thoughts, "These days it's possible to make it anything."

"So this isn't Vanga's phone?" asked Adie, almost disappointed.

The man ignored Adie's question. "Just imagine her in that position, arse in the air, jabbing under her bed with her rolling pin, trying to get her jaw out from under it." He broke again into loud, rude laughter that was so contagious Adie could not resist joining in.

"You shouldn't look at the phone anymore, anything could be written there," said the man on the line, as if he had read her thoughts."

"So, this isn't Vanga's phone."

"Only imagine her bending down and poking about with her rolling-pin to reach her false teeth," said the man instead of answering her and burst out in loud, hiccupping laughter that infected her and she also started giggling.

She began to wake up. For a few moments she could not work out where she was nor what was happening, she just carried on laughing. She hovered a little on the border, then crossed the line between dreaming and reality. Adie realised that she was in her bed and was soon wide awake, but the dream had been so vivid, it still had hold of all her senses.

Adie figured out that she had been awakened from a dream by the sound of her own laughter, but the phone conversation still seemed so real. She reached under her pillow and pulled out her phone to check ... but there was no VANGA listed.

"Well," Adie reasoned, "how could Vanga possibly be there? I've never added her to my contact list!" Adie's thoughts were now rational, though her first action had been far from clever. She put the phone back under her pillow and began to replay the dream in her head. It made her smile again. She was able to recall everything clearly: the ringing of the phone, the display lighting up with VANGA in capital letters, and the whole conversation, word by word.

"Pretty crazy!" was all that Adie could make of it. "But I far prefer this dream to that nightmare with the monster." She remembered, about a week ago, a hairy monster surging out of a dark lake and devouring at least twenty people, which Adie had witnessed close up and in gory detail.

"Crazy! Crazy! Crazy! I'd be better going back to sleep and leave the thinking for tomorrow" Adie decided. Turning onto her belly, she fell asleep again in a moment.

Adie did not often have dreams, but when she did they almost always awakened her. Her dreams were tightly intense, vividly detailed, and unusually bizarre. She hated the nightmares; it was difficult to fall asleep again after being woken up, sometimes in tears even, gasping in panic and with a thundering heartbeat that took her ages to soothe. What really angered her was that she remembered the nightmares for a long time, often for years.

There was a time when Adie believed that all dreams had a hidden meaning, a message to be interpreted. For a while, she had studied stacks of books about interpreting dreams, but soon she realised it was just wasting her time. Nobody could answer all of her questions. She could only agree, to some extent, with the thoughts of Freud, that dreams serve to satisfy needs that are unmet in reality; not only sexual needs, every need.

Adie remembered well how one evening she had badly craved some chocolate, but there was not a single piece in the house. That night she dreamed of a huge bar of fruit and nut chocolate that she ate secretly, so she didn't need to give it to anybody. That illustrated just about all, Adie felt, that could be understood about dreams.

And yet, this could explain only a small portion of all dreams, and mostly it applied to children's dreams. For her own allegorical dreams, Adie could find no explanation that satisfied her. She had placed the whole topic in a mental folder labeled:

'Do not try to cram the sky into your head, or your head will blow up!'

To this folder, Adie would consign all events for which she could find no rational explanation from this world.

For example, at one time when she was a student, far away from home with no money and starving hungry, she had said, "If I find 5 leva[16] on the ground in front of me right now, then I will believe that God exists." She looked downwards right after saying those words, and there on the street, just in front of her, lay 5 leva . Utterly staggered, Adie went and hit her head against a tree, but the money was still there. She took it, and her best friend, to a cafe where they stuffed themselves with food, like kids in a candy store. In those days you could do that with just 5 leva!

As she opened her eyes for the second time that morning, Adie remembered the dream. Fully awake, the story of the old woman and her jaw seemed even more ridiculous. Adie couldn't help but laugh at it. Her laughter almost choked her as she drank her morning coffee. That was the moment her man entered the kitchen. His face was a question mark. So Adie told him the story, in much the same way as the man of her dream last night, complete with hiccups of laughter.

"So, you are as crazy when you sleep as when you're awake?" observed her partner, but he also had to laugh.

Walking down Magic Alley on her way to work, Adie wondered about Vanga's involvement in this dream.

Despite all the condemnations of the prophetess that she had heard while she was a theology student, Adie respected Vanga and refused to see her as the witch the Orthodox institution denounced her as. But neither did she think that Vanga was a saint, as the populace proclaimed her. For Adie, Vanga was a true phenomenon, just as every man and woman should be, and probably would be at some time. What made Vanga phenomenal was her natural ability, without using any special techniques, to access that place in which everything is experienced as a connected whole. In other words, reality.

Adie had no doubt that Vanga helped some people to make better choices. Yet, Adie felt uncomfortable about Vanga's 'prophecies'. Such a concept did not sit well with her own values and beliefs. To her, anything that bypassed free choice seemed manipulative.

Of course, there are situations in life (and Adie had experienced her

---

[16] The lev is the currency of Bulgaria.

share of them) when there seems to be no escape from total confusion. At such times our greatest desire is for someone else to assume responsibility, to hold our hand and tell us what to do next and what will happen. But Adie had come to realise that this only happens when a person searches for answers from outside of themselves, rather than from their own inner essential being.

Alexey had pointed out to her that from the position of our essence, our potential, everyone could understand what was most important for them and could make the right choice. This simple truth had been illustrated in a very understandable way in the story of The Little Prince[17]. Of course, having made the right choice, taking the required action then demands courage, which is quite another matter.

Absorbed in these thoughts, Adie arrived at her desk in the office and turned on her computer. As she flicked the switch, she decided to dismiss the question of why Vanga had rung her in her sleep. For the sake of her sanity, she settled on a plausible explanation that it was probably to tell her to be more relaxed and less serious about things: see things more like a funny story about an old woman who sneezed out her jaw.

Satisfied with the explanation, Addie spontaneously said to herself 'Makumba'! This caught her off guard, so she then did what Alexey had specially warned them not to do: she Googled Makumba, although she expected no results. Adie's eyes widened in surprise. The word did exist. It meant 'auspice'. She read further, intrigued.

Makumba is a Brazilian Afro-Christian syncretic sect. At its core it is the main religion of the population of Brazil, although the majority of Brazilians, including the followers of Makumba, are Catholics. The cult itself has been banned for a long time. Makumba is a polytheistic religion, its pantheon of gods headed by the goddess of water, Yemanja, whose birthday is celebrated on January 1st.

Adie stuffed her mouth with her hand to suppress a cry of surprise. "This is already too much", she told herself.

Years ago, Adie had worked with an eccentric Brazilian guy. She could never decide for sure whether he was a devil or an angel, though he had a

---

[17] The Little Prince - first published in 1943, is a novella and the most famous work of the French aristocrat, writer, poet and pioneering aviator Antoine de Saint-Exupéry (1900–1944).

human body, of course. For some reason, he had liked Adie very much from the outset of their acquaintance. He would talk to her for ages, both about simple things in life and deep philosophical issues.

He loved to tell her about Brazil. With drawings, he had illustrated to her that the most beautiful female form was found in Brazil: a combination of flat European and lavishly curved African roots. He had told Adie about the beaches of Rio de Janeiro, about the favelas, about the music and the samba; about voodoo.

Once he even invited Adie to join him at night at a secret place by the river, to show her voodoo. Adie had just laughed. She never really knew whether he was serious or making these things up, but she chose to believe the latter.

He had also told Adie about Yemanja, the goddess of water. He had proclaimed henceforth, every year on January 1st when celebrating the birth of the goddess Yemanja, he would also celebrate the birth of the goddess Adie. He assured her that soon the goddess would be born in Adie. She needed just a little more time, he had said.

Though their paths had long parted, they had remained friends and still called each other on the phone. From time to time, he would find ways to send her a gift, a book usually.

As Adie sunk deeper into her memories, she began to wonder whether there might be some connection between what she had just read, her Brazilian friend and her elusive calling; he had, after all, given her the name Yemanja. "Maybe I really should have listened to him?"

Adie recalled that, many times, he had urged her to come to live in Brazil. "If you come, you will never want to go back. I will help you!" But Adie had never regarded his offer as a serious option. Brazil was too far away for her emotionally, not just geographically.

"How silly of me," she sighed with nostalgia, her hand still stuffed against her mouth. "He tried to loosen a little the noose around my neck, but I insisted on keeping it tight."

Adie returned to the Internet and continued reading the text on her screen:

Makumba attaches particular importance to the healing of the spirit. According to the beliefs of Makumba, the divine instills healing in the devotee who has passed through all the challenges it sets. As a result, this devotee leaves their previous life entirely and is born anew.

"Gosh!" exclaimed Adie under her breath. She continued in her thoughts, "This is where I am right now in my life, just like I'm deep in a Makumba ritual. I am looking for healing. I want to shed the load I carry in trying to conform to my ideas of the socium. I want to be born again, in my essence. If finding this is just coincidence… well, then I don't know what to believe any more."

"Look at what you have done!" Adie accused herself, and continued her self-prosecution relentlessly, "You destroyed an opportunity that might have taken you closer to your calling. Now you can only wonder whether you have screwed up the whole thing!"

Adie wondered. Could it be in Brazil, where perhaps her calling might be waiting for her? Or was she just projecting that idea from what she'd heard recently in a radio interview with that Portuguese fado singer?

The singer had said that fado means 'destiny' and that she had found it to be truly her destiny. Following that, Adie had learned about the correlation between fado and suadade, the permanent state in which a soul seeking its fado is immersed. Adie knew that in Brazil, the country of Makumba, suadade was officially celebrated thirty days after the birth of Yemanja. And, someone had once told her, she herself could be Yemanja…

Adie interrupted these shocking, mysterious connections as she suddenly realised that they were only her own creation, constructed by her own logic. She realised that there was no practical way to really know, in a Universe of such complex intertwining, whether there was any inherent meaning in her dressing of definitions, categories, forms.

Adie leaned back on her chair. She felt upset with herself, and angry. She just stared numbly at the computer screen… until someone slammed the office door.

She rose and went outside for a stroll, to clear her head of its fantasies. She decided to call a friend on her cell phone, someone she could rely on to be down to earth.

"Hey, do you have a minute?" asked Adie when her friend answered.
"I have much more than a minute," was the response.

Encouraged, Adie asked directly to the big question, "Sorry if this sounds strange, but can you tell me what you see me as?"

Her girlfriend probed a little, unsure what Adie was looking for, "How do you mean?"

"Well, let's say as a profession. I can't decide what I want to do. I can't find my calling," specified Adie.

"Oh, Adie, you philosophise so much!" said the girlfriend.

Now it was Adie who did not understand. "What do you mean?"

"Well … you are doing so many different things. You know, most people envy you for what you have already achieved and for what you are still doing now. Your life seems so interesting. I can't understand what else you're looking for," explained the girl friend.

"Maybe that's how it looks from the outside," agreed Adie. "Actually, I do find my own life interesting too, but what I can't find is any meaning to it all. Have you found your meaning yet?" she asked her friend.

"Oh, you dig too deep into things!" admonished her friend. "I am just fine with things as they are."

"You never wanted anything else? You never feel that something is missing?" Adie persisted.

"Well, I do have such moments from time to time, but they pass," the girlfriend admitted.

"For me, they don't pass. Quite the contrary; it keeps getting worse!" Adie's voice betrayed deep sadness.

"You okay?" the woman asked.

Adie picked herself up by returning to her first question, "Okay, okay, never mind. Please tell me what you see my calling as?"

"Well… I don't know. You already do everything that I can imagine that you would do. I can't imagine anything else. Maybe if you started doing something else, then I could see you as that, but right now I cannot figure out what that might be because you are so unpredictable!" Her girlfriend finished with a smile in her voice.

Adie remained silent.

The girlfriend tried to help further. "Perhaps the meaning is in the very search for meaning itself, as someone put it?" she offered.

"Yeah, yeah!" reacted Adie, and with irony added, "I imagine when I die and go to heaven they will ask me What have you been doing all your life? and I'll tell them I was looking for the meaning of it. How they will laugh their heads off!"

Her friend laughed. "I'm sorry I'm not a great help," she apologised.

"No, quite the reverse. Thank you for listening! I shall leave you to your work now, and I'd better get on with mine, too … until I find my meaning!"

They both laughed again, said goodbye and hung up.

Seated back at her computer, Adie questioned herself, "Why have I presumed that someone other than me can tell me who I am and what I should do?" she thought with a deep sigh. She opened a new file and began to write the article she was supposed to be sending to a magazine by the end of that day. Though she did not feel she was quite on form, the writing absorbed her.

For Adie, creative writing was always deeply engrossing. For her, there was no greater pleasure than the process of playing with thoughts and language. It made her feel like the director of a film, like the leading actress, like a spectator… all at the same time. Her greatest delight was in surprising her readers, including herself. As Adie wrote, she was always keenly aware that anyone reading would not know what was coming in the next sentence, just as she herself often did not know what it would be, until she had written it.

Adie loved words. Every word. Each was a unique expression, and how she combined them formed a natural flow that would enchant her reader to stay with her until the end. Many had expressed their admiration when touched by Adie's writing style, whether it was an article, a letter, even a business report. Reading her writing was fascinating, moving, an authentic and intimate experience.

Though Adie loved writing, she wasn't inclined to write on any topic that didn't interest her. And she loathed deadlines. That was why she had never pursued a career as a journalist, and why she had soon ended her spell in PR.

Adie finished her article and emailed it to the editor of the magazine. Still twenty minutes to go until the end of the workday. Why not distract herself for the remaining time by reading her favourite online magazine? She was cheerily surprised to find that many new articles had appeared since her last visit. As usual, Adie clicked first on the link to the SPIRIT section. She felt her heart leap when the first title appeared.

How to Find your Life's Purpose in 20 minutes

Adie just rolled her eyes 360 degrees. Now she really did not know what to think. Twenty minutes was quite specific though. This was no ambiguous sign that needed decoding. This article was promising to reveal to her how to find her true calling … in just 20 minutes, the very amount of time that she had available right now. Adie was trembling as she hovered on the edge of the imminent fateful disclosure.

She slowly leaned forward, tense and acutely aware that at any moment she might snap like an overstretched rubber band. Her face was pale and serious, as if awaiting news whether she was to live or die. Adie began reading…

How do you know what the real purpose of your life is? It's not about your daily activities and responsibilities, nor even about your long-term goals. The question is, "Why are you here? What is the real reason for your existence?"

So far, this was exactly what Adie had been hoping for. She continued reading…

If you desire to find your true purpose, you must first empty your mind of all the false purposes that it was filled with. If you are willing to accept the truth about yourself, try this simple process that we offer you. The more you open yourself to this process, the faster you will see results and the more confident you will be in using it. Whatever your doubts, even if you think this is a waste of time, it will still work for you; it will take a little longer, that's all. Here's what you should do…

Adie held her breath as she read the neatly presented steps…

1. Take a blank sheet of paper or open a new file on your computer.

2. Write at the top: "What is the real purpose of my life?"

3. Write down the first answer (whatever it is) that comes into your head. It need not be a whole sentence. A short phrase or even one word is enough.

4. Repeat step 3 until you reach an answer that makes you want to cry. This is your true calling. And that's all you need to do!

It usually takes 15 to 20 minutes to clear your head of its clutter, and to work past socially imposed expectations of what you thought your purpose ought to be. Your forgotten memories will at first throw up many incorrect answers. But when the true answer finally appears, you will feel as if it came from a completely different source...

There was more, but Adie could not wait. Wasting no more time, she opened a new file on her computer and focused on the question:

"What is the real purpose of my life?"

"To write!" was the first response that came. Adie put this answer down to her activity just moments ago: writing that article. She hurriedly typed in the answer and swiftly turned her thoughts to other possibilities. Several quickly emerged. Adie dismissed them all, not even bothering to type them in. She immediately recognised them as not only false but impossible.

After 15 minutes Adie was ready to cry, but not because she had found her vocation, rather because she couldn't think of any further single thing, not even a false answer...

"Actually," Adie comforted herself, "I'm not confused at all. I clearly know what is not my vocation," she asserted while deleting the only answer that she had typed in. "Remember, just a few days ago 'something' gave me a hint that my lack of knowledge about my vocation isn't in itself a confusion, so I needn't try to organise it all through structured exercises like this one," she reasoned as she prepared to leave work.

Walking down her Magic Alley with her headphones on, Adie fell into despair.

"Exactly!" she reacted, as her ears were filled by the song *Here I Go Again*[18] ... *"Tho' I keep searching for an answer ... I never seem to find ... what I'm looking for..."*

---

[18] Song of the British hard rock group White snake, founded in 1957, by David Koverdale, the front man of the group Deep Purple.

She could not formulate exactly what she was feeling or why; she just knew that it was making her unhappy. Deadlock, frustration, sadness, despair, anger... a mix of negative emotions were tormenting her insides. All she wanted was to be alone, quiet and undisturbed, at least for a little while.

When she got off her bus, Adie passed the street she normally took home, straight to the small park by the nearby church. Despite it being already cold and dark, there were a lot of people around. Adie headed for an empty bench in the least prominent spot. She sat there and observed the people. Some ambled along with dogs, others walked briskly, some were out with their children, there were also young people having a beer together...

Adie's attention was drawn to two children standing under the light of a lamp. They stood facing each other. One pulled his tongue out at the other; the other responded likewise. The first leapt into the air; the other jumped in the same way. Then the first knelt down; his partner followed. Adie wondered what their next move would be... Obviously the child was wondering too, but in a moment as she was squatting, she lay down directly on the ground. The other child, without any hesitation, did the same.

At that moment, two women, the mothers of the two children, leapt up from a nearby bench. Up until then they had been sitting together in quiet conversation, but now they jumped up and cried out to admonish their kids in unison, like they had rehearsed it at least a thousand times.

Adie laughed. The performance of those kids reminded her of what Alexey had said about mirroring. "Mirroring is a very powerful tool. We use it to create a rapport with another person, so that our interactions become synchronised, on the same wavelength. Similarly, by mirroring it, we can create a rapport with the Universe and become synchronous with it."

At that seminar they had discussed different ways of mirroring and Adie had experienced for herself the powerful effects. While mirroring, she had coped with her phobia of pigeons. She had also experimented with its effects on another person, that time when she had tamed the cheeky old lady on the morning bus.

"How do I mirror a calling?" pondered Adie. No answer came to her. Her calling seemed too abstract at the moment to mirror it. Adie rose from the bench and headed towards home.

She was silent all evening, wanting very much for the silence to remain undisturbed. Her beloved partner, however, was in a different mood. He began telling her stories from the time when he had served in the army. Adie pretended to listen, mentally begging him to finish soon. Then something he said grabbed her attention: "plate-table guys".

These guys had to write the flight numbers of each aircraft caught by the radar, upon special vertical transparent maps: plate-tables. Those who tracked the flights were on the other side of the maps, so the plate-table guys had to write the numbers in mirror-image for them.

Adie perked up. She found a pen and tried out some mirror-writing on her paper napkin, under the supervision of her beloved. She had to write a word from right to left, with each letter facing backwards. She tested each new attempt by turning the napkin round and holding it up to the light to see if the word then read correctly.

When she was satisfied with her new skill in mirror-writing, Adie took a clean sheet of paper and carefully wrote upon it:

ƎИITꞀꞀAↃ

She was quite cheerful now. "See what signs I receive to guide me!" Adie thought to herself. She took her sheet of paper and carefully pinned it up on the wall opposite the mirror in the entrance hall. The reflection in the mirror now showed the word as it would read normally.

"There!" Adie thought, "Each time I look at myself in this mirror, it now mirrors my elusive vocation. Surely, the identity of my true vocation will now come to me." Adie prepared for bed, delighted with her discovery of a way to mirror her calling.

13. CHAPTER THIRTEEN

The next morning before leaving for work, Adie lingered in front of the mirror, contemplating the reflection of her calling and also her own reflected image. She stared, unblinking, at her own face, until the image in the mirror began to blur, then faded completely away. As she continued to stare at the spot where her face had been, her eyes filled with tears and she blinked. The image of her face immediately regained its normal features and Adie smiled at it.

This was one of the first methods Alexey had shown them for entering the zero-state. Until now, Adie had not remembered to use it, yet it was so easy. All it required was to focus the eyes intently on any chosen object. Soon the details of the chosen object would appear to blur into a homogeneous whole, with no separate image, no form, no feeling, no reality any more. Through doing this, the mind would empty and become ready to accept the installation of whatever might be submitted to it: a new image, new form, new feeling… a new reality.

"Maybe I could embed," Adie thought, "the feeling of joy that I shall experience when I discover my calling." She began to dance around in front of the mirror with a wide smile, waving her hands in the air, mentally cheering, "Hooray! Hurray!" She realised that from her side she was faking it, but the mirror was unable to make any distinction: whatever it reflected back to her could only be for real.

As she was about to step out of her home, Adie remembered her mobile phone: it was still in the bedroom. She went back for it. The very moment she placed her hand on the phone she heard a loud crash from outside, as if two cars had smashed into each other out on the boulevard, yet again. Adie opened her bedroom window and leaned out to see what had happened. Indeed, as usual, someone had tried to make an illegal U-turn in the busy traffic, unsuccessfully. Thankfully, the drivers were shouting at each other, which meant they were fine.

As Adie stretched up on her tiptoes to close the top handle of the window, her eyes were directed to the side of the building diagonally opposite. It carried a huge billboard on which was written…

I AM NOT SEARCHING
I AM FINDING

Adie remained motionless on her tiptoes, holding on to the handle of the window. However long that billboard had been there, it was as if she was seeing it for the first time. She did not see what it was advertising; she only saw that huge inscription of those words, as if they had appeared in just that moment, just for her.

At work, Adie diligently set about her tasks, but her eyes kept wandering to the clock at the corner of her computer screen. She could not wait for lunchtime, when she could call Alexey. She badly needed to tell him about this stream of seemingly random coincidences that been flowing through her life the past few days. She knew he habitually went to bed late, so it was best not to call him before lunchtime.

At 11:30 she could wait no more. She went outside her office and called Alexey on her mobile. It turned out he had long been up and about, he'd had things to do that morning. But they were done, so when Adie asked whether he could spare a minute for her, he replied, "I am completely at your service, Adie."

She began to pour out everything, trying hard to keep things in the same sequence they had happened. First, she told Alexey about Fado and saudade … the subsequent Brazilian thread with Makumba, the very same word that had come up that time when she had tossed her Princess doll in the air, complaining that she could find no calling for herself … then there was that bizarre dream with the phone call from Vanga … then her search for the meaning of Makumba, which had led her to Yemanja and the idea of spiritual rebirth… then watching those kids in the park mirroring each other … followed by listening to her beloved talking about plate-tables, which gave her the idea to reflect her calling in the mirror … and finally how, through forgetting her mobile phone, she had seen the inscription "I'm not searching. I am finding."

"What do all these signs mean, Alexey? Where do they lead me?" This was the thing bothering Adie, the reason she had called him.

Alexey listened quietly to Adie's monologue. She imagined him sitting smoking as he listened, with that encouraging smile of his. "Wow!" he spoke only when he was sure she had finished. "What interesting things that happen around you, Adie! But beware. Trying to decipher the signs could drive you deeper into such a problem that we will struggle to get you out of it! Do not search for signs, Adie. Rather, use the resources that they are revealing to you … it is you who is the one finding them…"

Adie interrupted, "I'm not searching. I am finding."

"Exactly! And as you begin to see your world resourcefully, you will see everything is just right…"

Adie interrupted again, spontaneously singing her favourite song[19] from her childhood.

Everything is just right:
The fishes are flying,
The grass laughs wildly in the puddles,
And boats are running fast.

But some see things as wrong.
They think we make a joke
When we play the game in such a way
and they try to turn the world upside down.

"We must make this song the official anthem of the group," Adie concluded.

Alexey had listened with a patient smile. "Very appropriate," he agreed.

Somehow, talking to Alexey had lightened her heart. Adie felt happy that she had someone to share these things with, otherwise they would be quite unnerving. She was no longer worried about her calling. Something had happened inside of her. The noose had loosened.

---

[19] A song from one of the classical children films in Bulgaria (1971) "Hedgehogs Are Born Without Spines" The movie is full of humour, cheerfulness, and great love for kids.

In place of her habitual fear and mistrust, she now felt an absolute confidence that she had already found what she had been searching so long for. Not that she actually had, but she felt as though she had.

With a sigh of relief, Adie asked Alexey, "What are you doing now?"

"I am painting one of those cotton sticks used for ear cleaning… painting it pink," he replied.

"Why?" asked Adie, most curious.

"Because something's gone wrong with my refrigerator. I decided I don't want to deal with repair men, so I came up with the idea of putting a pink ear cleaning stick on top of the fridge," Alexey explained, as if he was doing the most natural thing in the world for dealing with a malfunctioning refrigerator.

Adie laughed. Silently, in her mind she sang again.

But some see things as wrong.
They think we make a joke
When we play the game in such a way
and they try to turn the world upside down.

Then she proclaimed aloud her admiration for Alexey's resourcefulness. "I cannot imagine anything that might work better! Well, I won't distract you any further. We don't want your steaks to defrost. Shall I see you tomorrow?"

"Yes, we start the new group tomorrow, don't we?" Alexey replied.

"Yes. Until tomorrow, then." Adie hung up.

She returned to her seat in front of her computer, still smiling about Alexey's pink ear stick. She noticed there was a new message in her official email inbox. It was from the chief editor of the magazine for which she'd written the article the previous day. They'd known each other for some time, and occasionally even met socially. The email was brief:

Adie, the article is brilliant. You are very good at writing. Indeed, it seems that writing is your calling. Maybe it is time for you to think about developing further this talent that you possess. Shall we meet over a glass of wine to discuss talents?

"Indeed, it seems that writing is your calling." Those words made her heart jump, her stomach tighten, her skin tingle… She felt the chill of sweat on her palms and just knew she had turned pale. Those words repeated in her mind, over and over; they just wouldn't stop. The mantra triggered something inside of her.

A movie of chaotic scenes started to flash through her mind.

She saw Adie the child, apparently playing with buttons, but actually using them to represent characters for stories.

Then came the Adie the writer of a column in the local newspaper; people recognised her in the street and stopped to greet her.

Next, the Adie who had entered a Brazilian writing contest with an essay written in Portuguese; though she hadn't won, heaps of praise had followed, with many words of encouragement for her to continue developing her talent.

Adie from just one day ago appeared, the one who could think of no other response but 'writing' in the exercise to find her true purpose.

Adie in her first year at school, winning first prize for the short story she wrote…

Adie closing the first book she had ever read, and feeling the passion it had ignited that she too would one day write that same way…

The movie reeled on and on. It seemed to have no end.

The working day ended. Adie was walking slowly down her Magic Alley, that same phrase still repeating in her head, like her mind was a juke box with no off switch. She noticed something shiny in the grass verge. It was too far away to see what it was clearly in the falling dusk. Adie stepped through the grass and bent down as she approached the thing: a can opener, solid metal with wooden handles. It seemed too beautiful an object to have fallen by mere accident into such a place as this.

Adie crouched next to the object looking it over with admiration, just like the 9-year-old Pippi Longstocking when she was playing as a thing-finder. In her mind, Adie began to talk just like Pippi did, *"Oh, what a wonderful can opener. The world is full of things and really needs someone to find them. It seems today is my lucky day."*

Suddenly, just as at the moment when she had stumbled into the huge dog turd, just yards from this same spot, a phrase appeared in her head. Adie smiled widely, and without caring at all who might hear she said aloud, *"A can opener can open up all sorts of situations!"* She pondered whether to pick it up and take it with her, but decided she would leave it so other people could also discover this powerful tool.

Adie stood and stretched. Her heart felt like it now had wings, fluttering with joy. She strode briskly down her Magic Alley. In the headphones, her player pumped out the sounds of one of her favourite performances of the Goran Bregovic orchestra, the belly dance tune *Mashala, Mashala*[20]!

"Mashala, Adie!" she cried out to herself, grinning from ear to ear. Her soul started to sway and bend, following the enchantment of the wild Balkan tune. Her brains, after a short reasoning, decided that in the government of the Universe there certainly must be some great joker assigned to her case. With that it also surrendered to the pull of the rhythm that it was now being teased with, and in bursting exultation started snapping its fingers with all the passion it was capable of.

P.S. This was the tenth day since Addie, after tripping into the dog's turd, stepped on a piece of newspaper which read: Only 10 days left...

THE END

---

[20] "Mashala" in Turkish means BRAVO.

AFTERWORD

Yes, Alexey is real.

Some people ask me why he smokes and drinks? Well ... the answer is: Because he is real!

Polished gurus are just stereotypes that fascinate our minds. What is worse: we're not even aware of the manipulation. We end up under the illusion that if we do everything "right", in a certain guru's way, then we will become like them, and will start living a super-life filled with happiness, harmony, love and abundance ...

Unfortunately, the promise of happiness almost never materializes as prescribed. Disappointed, we usually start blaming ourselves for being dummies, not capable of sticking precisely to the wise man's instructions or learning 'the secret'.

Helloooo!...

As someone quipped sarcastically: *If The Secret¹ is for real, then where is my Ferrari?*

OK. What is true is that the problem is not the Ferrari. Everybody can own a Ferrari, if that is what they really want.

The secret is that there is no 'secret'. There is no recipe or nostrum for overnight success. There is no universal remedy that can be applied to all and sundry like over-the-counter prescription drugs.

There exists an infinite, inexhaustible potential in all of us, to dig deep within and find the beauty in every situation, to make the most out of the circumstances we find ourselves in, and to emerge victorious in spite of everything, this is the task at hand - this is life.

Alexey is 100% Alexey. Only with such an Alexey can you remain original, be yourself and start the onward journey. Alexey shows you how to use what you already have, even if you are unaware of its existence. Alexey isn't varnished and he has helped many restore their connection with themselves, with the potential and live a miraculous life.

Many people have asked me about Adie – is she 'real' … Let me put it this way: while reading the book if you feel a close connect or you happen to know someone who is just like Adie – then the answer is 'Yes!'

What will happen to Adie? Will she be able to purse her vocation as a writer? Or will she fall hostage to the 'matrix' once more? This depends on her.

And so is the case with you, your life and your destiny is in your hand.

Alexey often says: *"I can take you to the corner only. From there on, it's up to you …"*

I sincerely hope you 'take the next step', experience the excitement and discover sooner rather than later that - 'Life Can Be a Miracle'.

Wishing you happiness!

Ivinela Samuilova

P.S. What about the seminars mentioned in the book? They are quite popular in Bulgaria. People have become more flexible intellectually and are not willing to adhere to a straight-jacketed way of life. In Alexey's approach, they find what works for them, they learn to use their inner and outer resources in the most appropriate way, and this helps them connect with the world outside in ways they never thought possible.

[1]It refers to the popular American movie *The Secret*, which offers a universal algorithm for attracting money, prosperity, success, happiness, etc.

ABOUT THE AUTHOR

Ivinela Samuilova was born on April 10th, 1971 in the town of Sevlievo, Bulgaria. She graduated from the University of Veliko Turnovo in Bulgaria with Master degree in Theology.

She also has degrees in Journalism and Psychology. She speaks English, Spanish and Russian languages. For some time, Ivinela used to work as a radio journalist in her hometown. In 2005 she moved to Sofia, the capital of Bulgaria.

In 2009 Ivinela wrote her debut novel 'Life Can Be a Miracle'. It has brought an unusually optimistic breath of fresh air, as warm as the Balkan summer, to Bulgarian literature. Having said that it would be appropriate to add that 'Life Can Be a Miracle' is a book without borders, as it speaks to the universal human spirit.

Other books by Ivinela Samuilova include 'If Life is Not a Miracle' and 'The Woman Who Sought Love.'

In order to satisfy her various interests, in 2007 Ivinela founded "Claritas Foundation", whose main activity is to preserve and promote Bulgaria's unique folk music heritage.

Ivinela's books turned out to be a phenomenon in the Bulgarian book market. Her novels have depth and character, touch readers with their sincerity, spread contagious vitality, and are claimed by readers to work as a therapy - lifting their spirits and inspiring them to look at life as a wondrous adventure.

In Bulgaria, Ivinela Samuilova is considered to be an influential, original and spirited new voice. Her writing style is easily distinguishable: intelligent, straight, witty, sincere and very refreshing.

Ivinela Samuilova loves to delve into the inner world of a human being and its relationship with Creation, the World and everything that surrounds it. This is what occupies most of her time.